THE WALL
OF SMOKE

A NOVEL

By

James L. Wolf

Publisher's Page

Author's Note

Writing this narrative has brought home the many rewards of family love. Foremost, Marcella, my wonderful wife, and her gift of life in our children; Justin, the epitome of motivation; Joseph, who created a new definition of determination; and Anna, a constant source of inspiration to all.

Dedicated

To

The memory of

Ben Lincoln

And

His stories

THE TWIN RIVERS
RESERVATION

❧

THE YEAR: 1996

12/1/12

Stuart Breger

Thank you,

Jam I. Wolf

CHAPTER 1

Miguel Alonzo's sense of foreboding had gradually increased from the moment Woodson's truck had crossed the cattle guard from the highway into his front yard, some fifteen minutes ago. When he had heard the rumble of the rails on the crossing, like a drum roll on his ribcage, he was out of bed, into his pants, and at the front door before Woodson and his prosthetic leg could reach the doorbell, waking his family. The illuminated dial said 4:05 a.m.

"There is Bad Blood at Lodge and Katy's house, bad, bad blood." Woodson Pino, pale with fright, spoke in the whispered click of his guttural Navajo.

Mother of God, Bad Blood, what a foreboding threat to wake up to, Miguel thought. Wanting to kick the hell out of Woodson was Miguel's first reaction, thinking him drunk or blown out of his mind on glue, paint, or some other hallucinogen, all of which Woodson had been arrested for in the past.

Stepping around the screen door into the coolness of the desert morning, Miguel pulled Woodson close, smelled his breath, and turned him towards the lights from his pickup. A wild fear emanated from his eyes. He led Woodson off the porch steps, walking lightly on the small, sharp rocks with his bare feet. Like a hissing valve, he whispered, "Now

Woodson, let's hear this again. Did you say someone was dead at Lodge's?"

Woodson nodded his head yes and repeated, "Bad, bad blood."

Miguel, with a determination that even the devil would recognize, ordered him, "Wait. Wait right where you are."

Diane, his wife, had seen her husband called out on emergencies many times. Tonight, however, she sensed his urgency just by the number steps he took between the porch and the bedroom. Also, he checked the readiness of his gun before slapping it into the holster. Their eye contact in the shadowed light from the vehicle in the yard carried the emotion that filled both of them in these moments. As softly as possible, Miguel stepped out of the bedroom. He heard her whisper the Navajo words, "Be careful."

Woodson, fearful and trying to stop his shaking, began to wander in a circle, stomping his cowboy boots in the rhythm of the hitched step caused by his wooden leg, mumbling in Navajo. At the same time, he pulled his head down into the collar of his blue denim jacket and his hands tucked up under his armpits, as if the cool desert breeze was an arctic blast.

Although he understood Navajo somewhat, Miguel could not understand what Woodson was saying. In an effort to quiet him, Miguel entered Woodson's dancing circle and grabbed his jacket from the rear, pulling him to balance on the prosthetic leg. Miguel then put his Pancho Villa mustache to Woodson's ear and tried to shock him with a fierce voice. "Shut up, Woodson. You'll do exactly as I tell you. Nothing more. Nothing less. Got it?" Fearful of being dropped on his ass, Woodson's head wobbled an assent. Miguel put him back on his good leg. "Now, I'll follow you back to the housing area. We'll talk up there. When you get there, you stay in your truck. Is there anyone else at Lodge's house, as far as you know?"

Calming down somewhat under Miguel's firm tactics, Woodson imitated Miguel's tone and whispered, "No, I don't tell no one. I come right here." Woodson fumbled his way around the hood of the truck. He grabbed the open door and, in an acrobatic move, threw himself up behind the steering wheel, using the wooden leg like a pole vault pole.

Miguel needed no such leverage to put his small, five-foot-eight-inch-frame into the tribal Suburban. The engine responded immediately and he waited for Woodson to move. As Woodson's truck circled the yard back to the cattle guard, Miguel turned on the radio and tried to raise the tribal police station in Battlefield, on the big reservation, 250 miles south of the Twin Rivers. Nothing.

He knew that that would likely be the case because the radio relay station on Mount Taylor had been struck by lightning almost two weeks ago. Cell phones were still useless here on the Twin Rivers Reservation. Land lines were still a dream. He would figure out a way to get some backup assistance after he got up to Lodge's and learned more about the Bad Blood that had frightened Woodson so deeply.

Woodson was out of the yard and about of a quarter of mile up the hill before Miguel put the Suburban into gear and replaced the radio microphone, all with one sweep of his arm. The panel clock read 4:33 a.m. Even though there was no traffic on the only paved road through the reservation, the shimmy in the frontend of Woodson's truck would keep him under fifty-five miles per hour. The five miles to the housing project, at this rate, would take about eight minutes. Strange, he thought, how little things made up his relationship with the people in such a small community, even the condition of their vehicles. Although not part of the culture, he was a part of reservation life. He felt safe with that distinction. The Suburban quickly caught up.

Bad Blood had only one meaning in Navajo, Miguel thought to himself. Death, and not just any death. It was a family death, a death related to the long-standing ill will and hatred among the extended families, a death related to the dark spirits which, more often than not in the form of a skin walker, came out of the mountains at night.

In the past, Miguel's Spanish heritage, like a shoreline beacon, had guided him in moments like this. It had told him that what the Navajos believed was real for them but not necessarily for him; and if he crossed cultural lines from his Spanish roots, then things could really get messed up. During the past three years as a tribal police officer he had learned that if he kept to what he was, his mind could work these matters out. Then, with the unconscious reference of a nicotine user, he tapped his breast shirt pocket and put the first pinch of snuff in his lower lip.

"Woodson, are you sure it was Bad Blood that you saw in there?" Miguel asked. Woodson could only shake his head. Miguel had pulled the Suburban up behind Woodson and was now standing by the side of Woodson's truck in the brightness of the Suburban's lights. Looking at him, Miguel sensed an almost paralyzing fear in Woodson. The whiteness of Woodson's knuckles on the steering wheel, his bulging neck muscles, his unwillingness to look at the darkened house, and the manner in which he twisted his body away from the direction of the house all confirmed the fear associated with Bad Blood.

What is more, Woodson's eyes seemed to have been swallowed into the sockets behind the high cheekbones of his pallid face; he did all that he could to make the bill of his baseball cap act as a shield against some force apparently emanating from the front door of Lodge's house. From this tortured expression, Miguel concluded that Woodson was close to losing it altogether and that there was no use now in asking him what he had seen or how he had seen it.

Miguel Alonzo hesitated at Lodge's front door as though it were an immoveable object. Slowly, he began to move through that moment of inertia caused by the foreboding of Bad Blood. His hand reached for the doorknob. He paused again and then stopped. Reaching behind himself, he pulled his gloves from the back of his utility belt and slipped them on. Strangely, he reflected, the uncertainty that awaited him on the other side of the door was not a personal threat. Woodson's fear had not transferred to him. He felt no need to draw his pistol. He turned the knob and walked into the small hallway that led to the living room.

The wave of stench that met him as the interior air began to move toward the opening of the door literally drowned any sense of expectation. Involuntarily, he folded in the middle, turned, and threw himself backwards out through the door's opening. The fluids of a now empty stomach made their way up and out of his throat, pushing the fragments of snuff out his mouth and nose.

Hanging over a small railing, he took a long moment to collect himself, the regurgitation messing his shirt and right trouser leg. Fortunately, the tobacco in his nostrils had also cut off the combined smell of blood, urine, feces, smoke, and alcohol coming from the hallway door. Miguel knew that he would have to get some air circulating before he could go into that house.

Instinctively, he moved toward the back of the house, making his way around the west side, the living room side of the house. Because he lived in one, he knew that all tribal housing had the same basic floor plan. He also knew that if there was enough light he should be able to see the front half of the living room floor through the west window. Nothing. His flashlight did not help because the back of a sofa blocked the lower half of the window.

As Miguel rounded the corner of Lodge's house, next door, Dan T. Begay was standing on his front porch, watching the events next door unfold as if he were the director on a movie set. With full authority, he moved down the steps towards Miguel.

"Stay where you are," Miguel shouted in Navajo. Putting the light into Dan T.'s face, a face so stoic that it could have been chiseled from the reservation sandstone, Miguel repeated the same message in Spanish and English. And then, in the hope of scaring him back into the house, he spoke the one Navajo word for Bad Blood. With that news, Dan T. turned back up the steps and shut the door behind him. Miguel was sure that the face in the lighted window of the house across the street had also heard his message to Dan T. Within moments, the entire housing project would have the words, Bad Blood. While the phrase literally stopped Dan T. in his tracks, Miguel wished that he had not said it.

Lodge's new pickup stood within a foot of the back stairs, protecting the passageway like a mechanical predator waiting for prey. Miguel was all business now. In the last few seconds, his life as a professional tribal policeman had clicked in. He approached the partially open back door and kicked it back. Others had apparently used their feet in the same manner, because its lower panels were broken and it swung in on the one nail in a single hinge connecting it to the doorframe. He flipped the hallway switch. A dim light responded from a bulb hanging by a wire in the middle of the small hallway. The light fixture was long gone and exposed the opening in the plywood behind it.

On his right, firewood was stacked between the inner and outer doors. He had to step to the left and over two worn truck tires and a toolbox that apparently had recently fallen off a broken shelf, scattering its wrenches, sockets, and screwdrivers in every direction. He got to the kitchen door and pushed it open. Immediately, the draft of air flowed from behind him and with a satisfied sigh, he knew that he could now work his way into the house.

Images that made up the kitchen registered as nothing out of the ordinary. The light flashed across dirty dishes in the sink, the velvet picture of "The Last Supper" on the wall, the cabinet doors missing over the sink, the drawers hanging out, and the linoleum that was torn and worn through to the concrete floor at each doorway leading from the kitchen. It all belonged. He stopped at the doorway into the living room. With his light, he caught the outline of two naked bodies across the doorway leading out of the living room into one of the adjoining back bedrooms. In a single motion, he turned out the light and dropped to his knees. With a hand on his pistol, he listened for the eternity of one moment. Nothing. Standing, he reached his hand around the corner and put on the living room light.

At no time in his life had he ever witnessed the quantity of blood that lay on the living room floor. He had witnessed accidental death numerous times, on the highways, in the fields, and in the Hogans with dirt floors; but this was a first for him. He was now in a home where the blood swelled up in a giant pool because it could not reach the earth.

The dead lay in a position of making love, grotesque against the background of their own blood. At this distance, Miguel could see that the top of the man's head was missing, as his face lay cradled between her breasts.

Even with the fresh air, the realization that he was looking at the remains of Lodge and Katy Tom caused the stirring of his stomach reflex once again. But this time it was controlled. He turned and walked back through the kitchen and out to the Suburban.

CHAPTER 2

*North Chapel
Monday, 5:00 a.m.*

Lodge Tom's grandfather, Fabriano Tom, now seventy-three years old, sat hunched over at the side of his bed located under a lean-to of cedar posts and pinion branches attached to his Hogan. Fully dressed, he reached for his boots at the end of the bed. In silence, he honored the great transition from night to day. The stars were still visible as he looked up through the pinion needles. The sun, in brilliant red, was rising in the east, etching the silhouette of the Cibola Mountains across the horizon. Pinion Valley, below him, still lay hidden and silent in the moment before the darkness flees. The mesa behind became the target for the first rays of the sun. The sheep and goats stirred inside the corral at the edge of the family compound.

With the exception of severe weather, Grandfather had lived his entire life under the sky hovering over his desert mountain land. The wrinkles on his hands and face were as countless as the crags on the face of the mesa behind him; his knuckles and feet like the pebbles on the ground. His color was that of the parched desert mountains. According to his belief, man came from the earth and returned to it. Grandfather believed that the return to the earth was a privileged step, taken each day, and the closer you joined the earth, the more human you became. This was the privilege of every man, woman, and child.

The earth contained all the men, the women, the children, and the beasts of the past. They were still there. One needed only to learn to read their signs. Could he not follow a deer or a lost sheep for days? He was able to tell exactly what the animal was feeling by the sign it left on the earth. And so it was with people, past and present. Their signs were likewise on the earth. No one passed through life without impressing upon the earth signs of his or her passage. Of those who left the earth, the wise ones, whom he hoped to join very soon, made their spirits available to the people during their time of need.

Much of the support for Grandfather's life flowed from his own father and the signs that this wonderful man had embedded in the earth's clay. Had not his father constructed the Hogan behind him from the earth's soil turned into adobe? Each winter, the mud and logs of the ceiling put into place over a hundred years ago still sheltered and protected him from the cold, the snow, and the rain. The shape, the size, and the strength of the livestock corrals where he put his sheep last night, although expanded, were the original limbs and brush that his father had carried down from the mesa.

His father had brought water to the earth's surface by digging some forty feet deep within the earth, solely with the strength of his hands. This act had succored life for five generations. And then, not least, there was himself, the last of his father's personal signs for all to read. What further signs had awaited creation by his father? No one would ever know because his father's horse had fallen in a prairie dog hole. He was taken back to the earth from which he had come by a horse that had to die with him.

Grandfather's wandering thoughts, like a movie, took him back to the days when he was a young man, when the Bible men came to the reservation. The Bible was never really his teacher, rather, it had stories about what he had already learned. When the first preachers came to the Pinion Valley, they were white men just like the first Bureau of Indian Affairs government agents. In fact, they came only months apart. Their words were the same. Their promises were the same. And their lies the same. In all these new relationships, he followed his mother's advice: *Listen respectfully even though you cannot understand their tongue. Say nothing, and then go and find your life on the earth.*

Later, the Navajos from the other Navajo reservations came with the same Bible. At least then, he could understand the language of the preachers. The part he loved was the creation story, the story about a god breathing into the earth and making man. These events sounded similar to what he had heard from his grandfather, who had died with what he considered a great privilege: His grandfather had never in his life spoken to a white man. But now, Fabriano Tom realized that his morning meditation had lasted too long. He must get ready for today.

When the dawning light reached the bottom of the mesa, his granddaughter, Tanya, Lodge's half-sister, would have breakfast ready for him. Her tribal house was one of ten dwellings in what the BIA agents referred to as the Tom compound. The Navajos called the place North Chapel, after the church that was completed five years ago. It had been twenty-five years in the making. The cross on top now reflected the morning's red sun against the night's disappearing shadows.

Tanya greeted her grandfather in the traditional manner, her slight frame bearing the correct angle to show deference and respect. Their hands gently touched. She had placed a bowl of steaming oatmeal and a cup of black coffee on the table. Beside it were a canteen of water and cellophane wrapper of wet blue cornmeal mush. These would accompany her grandfather as he took the sheep into the valley. Hunched over the table, he ate alone. Tanya sat silently, watching the new day through the eastern doorway of her wood-framed house.

She more than loved the old man. He was her life. For the past ten years, since she had quit work in Albuquerque and left her alcoholic man, Grandfather's presence and stories had given birth to an unparalleled peace and joy in her life. She had spent countless hours with him tending sheep in the valley. The apparent nothingness of those hours in the shade of a large sandstone or the overhang of dry creek bottom were filled by the men, the women, the loves, and the life of her grandfather's seventy-three years.

What traditional and cultural memories she now possessed! Medicines, stories, and ways that traditionally were passed on from man to man, her grandfather had passed on to her. Early on, he had warned her that she must be armed with the medicines of the People. Why her? His response to this question, posed at different times by older clansmen, remained the same: "Soon you will know."

Tanya did not have the traditional long, flowing hair of a Navajo. She dressed like any white person, in a T-shirt and sweat pants. She was a tiny woman at just under five feet tall. Her features were definitely Anglo, with fair skin, blue eyes, and soft cheekbones under a narrow forehead shadowed by short, brown hair.

Tanya was raised a Navajo, spoke Navajo, and after these years with her grandfather, knew the Navajo culture better than most people; but she was not accepted by the women of the reservation because her father had been a white man. So, also, were the fathers of her half-brothers, Lodge and Francis John.

She had come to learn from her auntie that their fathers had been three different cowboys from the Locus ranch south of Battlefield. When pregnant, their mother would come back to the reservation to have her babies. Within a few months after their births, she would return to the ranch and leave the children for the grandparents, aunts, and uncles to rear. This "parenting" was in exchange for the dollars that her mother would occasionally send to the extended family.

Early one summer morning, the three of them, Tanya, Lodge, and Francis, as teenagers, had met their fathers through a pair of binoculars. From a hillside north of the Locus spread, where they had driven before dawn over some sixty miles of unimproved roads, they had spent the morning looking down into the activities of the ranch's headquarters. Their mother lived in the main ranch house with the three owners. She freely went in and out. She cooked, did the washing, and cleaned for the men. And by noon of that day, Tanya knew that her father was Gus Dingles. Lodge's dad was Joe Lincoln. It was not until the cowhands came in to lunch that Francis John was able to identify his father, the ranch foreman, Matt Whiting.

Still in reverie about her family, Tanya stood up and leaned into the doorway, looking for a vehicle to clear the rise in the road and come into view. She had heard its motor groan through the Mountain Top pass and, out of habit, waited to see who was heading north out of the reservation at this early hour. Her heart constricted with a deadly fear that crawled across her breasts as she followed the Suburban's slow turn into the Toms' compound of homes. There enough daylight behind Miguel for Tanya to see him lean out the window and spit the clot of snuff out of his mouth.

He eased the truck gently across the cattle guard and slowly drifted to a halt not fifteen feet from her doorway.

"Grandfather, it's Miguel."

The old white head, slowly moving from a position of alertness to one of sorrow, bowed even lower in acknowledgment of the inevitable.

CHAPTER 3

Like a molded cast, Miguel remained motionless for a very long moment. Literally aching to be away from this unfolding madness, he wished to heaven that he had failed the five-month training course for tribal policemen at the Navajo Academy in Window Rock. Today, being one of only six non-Indian Navajo tribal police officers meant nothing but pain. It was a good job on small reservation, or had been, until this morning.

The twenty-minute drive up to Tanya's home had, briefly at least, stemmed the flow of adrenaline. His clothing remained soaked from the previous hour's known and unknown tensions. Miguel was under no illusions. Tanya would know that something surely had happened to Lodge. Otherwise, as with previous emergencies, Lodge would be here, with him.

When Francis, their brother, died in an auto accident on Three Mile Curve, two years ago, Miguel had gone to Lodge. The same when Grandfather's brother, inebriated to unconsciousness, drowned in an inch of water just north of Saw Tooth last winter. Lodge was the family's shoulder. Now, there no longer was a Lodge. The mantle of despondency, despair, and dependence now belonged to Tanya. Miguel could see her small body stiffen to the same realization.

The three of them, Miguel, Lodge, and Tanya, had been inseparable at Saw Tooth High School. In fact, it was Lodge who ultimately discouraged Miguel's affection for Tanya, making him realize that Tanya had to marry a Navajo in order to stay on the Twin Rivers Reservation. The white man's blood in them did not affect Lodge's position with the Navajos. It did, however, negate Tanya's place among the women. It was Tanya who reluctantly had convinced Miguel to accept Lodge's warning.

Miguel knew he must not keep her waiting any longer. As he released his locked arms from the steering wheel, he similarly willed a new flow of energy from deep inside. His body failed to respond. Instead, as he pushed open the door, a streak of weakness felled him to his knees. Weaving between the door and the seat, as if his spine had disintegrated, he grabbed the door's armrest and slowly straightened up. Tanya, who had never lost her empathy for Miguel, grasped the severity of his situation and stepped out of the doorway towards him.

"It's Lodge, isn't it? How bad is it? Is he dead?" Each question contained the implied answer. Her voice lowered, gradually, to a deep-seated gasp.

Walking toward the doorway, with needles in every joint, Miguel simply nodded. *Miguel had decided that he would keep the worst to himself for the time being.* "He and Katy appear to have been shot to death."

Returning to the kitchen side by side, they both suddenly stopped, as if an invisible barrier had risen up through the floor. Their reactions were to a sound, a gentle, piercing, wail that rose from the other end of the room. As the rising sun cast their silent silhouettes across the threshold, they bowed to Grandfather's response to the news of Lodge and Katy's deaths. The death chant, which they both recognized, was Grandfather's way of telling them that he had heard, and more importantly, was preparing, in his way, for this latest of his family's tragedies.

When the chanting stopped, out of respect, they waited for the old man, who was now standing over the back of his chair. Without greeting Miguel in the customary manner of a gentle touching of the hand, he quickly moved around both of them, towards the open door. As he did so, he whispered a single Navajo word that meant, "I must know."

Although her mind raced with the intensity of her pounding heart, she remained silent with a refined acquiescence and accepted her grandfather's ways and words. He was entering a ceremonial phase that would prepare him and his family for Lodge's loss and, ultimately, his burial. He desired aloneness until the time he would again approach them.

Tanya looked at Miguel's strained face. She walked over to the window, working hard to sort out her own wave of confusion and anger. Conflicting faiths sought dominance while her mind swirled with questions, wanting simple, reasonable answers. Did Lodge's temper finally meet a stronger will? Two children from a previous marriage and their own little boy of five months, what was now in store for them?

Katy's first husband had also died of guns. Katy was the cursed one. Lodge would never acknowledge the need for a ceremony to cleanse Katy after that death. He tried to live the new religion with a god who spoke to them through the mouths of preachers and their signs of heavenly forgiveness. For Lodge, the preacher's words and hymns had replaced Grandfather and his humble signs from the earth. As she clasped her head, she swiped a plant from the windowsill, behind the sink. It fell and dumped dirt on the counter and down onto the floor, jarring her back to Miguel's presence. "I am sorry, Miguel. What happened? But, Good Lord, wait… where is the baby…where are the kids?"

"There were no children down there. According to Woodson, Willow Jr.'s woman has the baby. Lodge's older kids are with their mother in Saw Tooth." Lodge's former wife worked at the Bureau of Indian Affairs dorm in Saw Tooth.

Resorting to her common kitchen tasks gave Tanya another moment to gather herself. Picking up Grandfather's cup, she motioned him to the table. "Come over here, please." Pushing her short hair behind her ear, she went to the stove and poured him a cup of coffee. "Now tell me."

"There really isn't much more that I can tell you about their deaths, at least not right now. About an hour and a half ago, Woodson came to my house and told me of the Bad Blood at Lodge's house. I investigated and found the two of them." With a discernible lowering of his voice out of concern for Tanya and due to his own exhaustion, he whispered, "It is just god-awful." After a moment, getting back to the practical matters, he continued, "Right now, one of the Cuba County's deputy sheriffs is securing the scene. Fortunately, I was able to raise John Tilden on the Cuba radio. I waited there until he showed. He is making sure that nothing is disturbed at the crime scene and holding Woodson down there until I give him the signal to send him home. I didn't want Woodson to go back to the Pinos' compound until I got there first."

Tanya did not hear anything after Woodson's words, Bad Blood. She could never ever believe what Woodson Pino saw or said. He was an opportunist. Whatever had a dollar sign attached to it would be the guide for what Woodson would say or do. In turning out like he did, he was everything his parents could have hoped for. Receiving Social Security Income as the result of a motorcycle accident provided a basic family income. Who could be more fortunate? *God, I've got to stop these hateful thoughts.*

"Go do your work, Miguel . Come back when you can." She left him and went into the bedroom, too angry for tears of grief at the moment.

Loss. Always the loss! It could be loss in almost any terms: money, property, animals, land, parents, and now Lodge had been taken away. Where was the balance of life for herself or, for that manner, for any of her people?

Lodge, what happened? Was it Katy? Her family? The stories of Katy's unfaithfulness with the white doctor might have reached him. *I will find out if that story is true and then I will personally destroy that damn white man. Were we so far apart that you could not come and talk?* Navajo men must show no weaknesses in front of their women, nor should the women shame their men by asking. Maybe he had returned to alcohol?

She stood before her bedroom window long enough to notice that the sun was beginning to creep down the mud-filled logs of her aunt's Hogan next door. The Bad Blood stories, ugly and harmful, would now circulate throughout the reservation. Someone, in frenzied hatred, had had Lodge and Katy killed with bad spirits. The lines of family ties and relationships would be discussed, and accepted or denied, depending upon their usefulness to the individual.

Miguel continued to sit in the kitchen after she left for her bedroom. Reaching over, he took several slices of Rainbow bread, rolled each one up like a tortilla, and dunked it in his coffee. He needed a tortilla right now. He needed the safety of his Spanish roots, the smell of his barrio home in Saw Tooth, where he was born. Santa Maria, the simple act of eating never felt so good. It helped to reaffirm who he was in the face of the tragic events of the past hour and a half.

Walking out through the doorway, he paused in the full sun, letting its warmth orient his resolve to move on with his message of death. Leaving Tanya's coffee cup on the doorstep, he climbed back into the Suburban. Slowly, he eased the vehicle back over the cattle guard, across the paved road and down the dirt road that took him deeper into Pinion Valley. Pinos' Hogan was about five miles away on the far east side of the reservation.

CHAPTER 4

Green Mountain
Monday, 6 a.m.

*W*hen *in hell will it ever change?* Miguel thought. How many times had he, in his official capacity as a tribal police officer, been to the Pinos' Hogan due to the drunkenness, the beatings, the juvenile problems, the accident reports, the deaths? He really couldn't remember the number of times. This would be the second time, though, just for Katy's husbands. The first husband had shot himself to death, when was it—three years ago?—in his pickup over in the Mountain Top area? With Woodson's involvement in this mess, Miguel knew that he would have to again review the conclusions of that suicide and all of the circumstances surrounding it. This time, the journey of death to the Pinos wasn't just about Katy's husbands; it was about Katy as well.

Miguel was grateful for one thing, for the time alone during the drive. Tanya's reaction had so typified the stoicism of the Navajo women, hiding a broken heart in the tradition of self-effacement. It was so different from his mother's reaction when his older brother was killed in a hunting accident three years ago. She had spent the entire day before the statue of Mary, talking, complaining, praying, and weeping; leaving only when family or a neighbor appeared for a few moments. Cultural identity tended to rescue us in moments of such devastation. He wondered if Tanya would lead the

Navajo women in their one moment of public emotion, the traditional wailing of the dead.

The unimproved roads of the reservation brought screeches and moans from deep within the Suburban. Road maintenance was nonexistent, particularly on the road to the Pinos' Hogan, a dead-end road. As he made the sharp turns to avoid canyon-like ruts, Miguel reviewed the last two hectic hours.

Once back in the Suburban after entering Lodge's house, he had called for backup on the Cuba County sheriff department's radio unit. This was one of the first times that Miguel had used the unit to call them. Numerous times since the county had given the radio to him, the sheriff's deputy had called him about Twin Rivers people who were dead, arrested, or in some kind of trouble, like being drunk and needing a ride back to the reservation. But this time, after Miguel had told him what he had seen in the house, John Tilden replied that he was on his way and should be out there in twenty to twenty-five minutes. The law enforcement system would take over and all of the major agencies would know, within the next fifteen to twenty minutes, what Miguel had reported. It had relieved him no end to know that help was on its way.

Miguel had talked to Woodson while waiting for the Cuba County deputy sheriff. The official investigators would never believe Woodson. What an understatement! The police would think that the dog thing was just a cover-up. And maybe it was. Yet, in some ways, he felt sorry for the crippled man. The problems that he had overcome since his motorcycle accident were a real tribute to his strength and gutsiness. Hadn't he proved that a one-legged man could win a rodeo buckle for calf-roping? At the same time, the man, as though in a trance, just wandered from trouble to trouble with law-enforcement agencies on and off the reservation.

The fact that he had found these bodies and had also been the last person to see Katy's first husband alive could be more than just a coincidence. He reached down and rewound the tape of the conversation that he had with Woodson about an hour ago.

"Woodson, where is the baby?" he heard himself ask, again feeling the chill of cold sweat down his back as he remembered his anxiousness. Was their child, dead or alive, across that pool of blood, in one of the bedrooms?

"Willow Jr.'s." Woodson's stupor continued and the responses were only syllables.

"Woodson, what do you know about those bodies in there?"

No reaction to the mention of the dead people.

"Were you in there? Had you seen them?"

"I want to speak in Navajo," Woodson said. "Only a Navajo will know what I mean."

"Later, Woodson, for the Navajo." Strained with anger, Miguel somehow contained it and calmly continued, "Just give me whatever you can say in English. There are some things that I got to do right away. Do you hear me? I have no time for an interpreter right now. So, speak to me. I figure that you must have been here at least by 4:00 a.m. or earlier this morning to get back down to my house at the time you did. What was so important for you to be here at that early hour?"

"Lodge was going to pay me some money that he owed me." Woodson stuttered. "I left home early. Lodge is always up by 4:00 a.m., doing stuff. But this morning there was no light on. But I parked over there and went up to the house anyway. I saw what happened to you when you opened that door. I smelled it, too. But when I opened it, an animal came running out. It brushed by my wooden leg and threw me down, see? Look at this bump on my head. I got it from that post over there. You know what that is on my pants. It's blood. I got it on my hands; then, I wiped it on my shirt." The recorder went silent except for the bump, bump, bump as Woodson pounded his head on the truck's steering wheel. "Jesus, Miguel, it's blood from in there. What did you see in there? Is it Katy, Lodge? Somebody is dead, ain't they? Just like I said. And this is Bad Blood all over me. I know it is!"

"You mean to tell me that you were never in there? Let me see your feet." Damn it, he thought. I have to get back to basic instincts.

There was a pause in the recording. He had put the flashlight on Woodson's feet, pushed open the door, and run over to the front door for the second time. With his light on the small concrete stoop, he saw them. For god's sake, there they were: animal prints coming out of the house, with one set on the concrete where the animal had skidded and then, apparently, leaped off to the right, overlapping his own pool of vomit. Earlier, in his anxiousness and sickness, he had missed all of it. It just convinced him that he had to wait for the forensic people before doing anything more in that house.

Then, the recording continued:

"Where did that dog go? Which direction? It's got to be around here if it belonged to Lodge. Do you know?"

"I didn't say that it was no dog. Anyway, Lodge and Katy don't got no dog, Miguel. Only a Navajo will understand what it was. Bad Blood, Miguel." He was shouting and crying. The recording was only a screech as Woodson's shouts surpassed the recorder's capacity.

"Come on, Woodson. Don't give me that shit." He too had shouted. Another piercing sound on the recorder substituted for his harsh, angry words.

Miguel's frustration with Woodson's account lingered in the air of the Suburban, just as if Woodson were still sitting next to him. He reached over and shut off the recorder. Woodson had begun to shake again, this time so badly that it was useless to continue the conversation. They had sat in silence, waiting for Tilden. When the deputy finally arrived from Saw Tooth, Miguel told him to keep Woodson there until he radioed back from the Pinos' house, probably in about an hour. "John, keep the people the hell out of here. Rope it off or something, somehow."

Now, an hour or so later, he reached over for the microphone and got Tilden on the radio. "I am on my way to the Pinos. Release Woodson, if you think that he can drive. Be sure and tell him to come straight home to his parents' place."

Margery and Willow Sr. sat outside of their Hogan drinking coffee and waiting, as was their custom when they saw the dust of a vehicle coming down their road. Visitors would stop their vehicles right in front of them. On this occasion, Miguel rolled down the window as Willow stepped over to him cursing in a jumble of Navajo words. Miguel recognized from the tone that there would be no customary greeting. On the contrary, he sensed from the old man's voice that, for whatever reason the police came—and they had come often—and regardless of what he had to say to them, Miguel was at fault. He had caused the looming hardship just because he was here.

When Willow stopped, Miguel began, "Woodson is on his way home right now, but Katy and Lodge won't be coming home anymore." Miguel then eased out of the truck, walked over to a log that had been brought to the house for firewood, and sat down. Respect called for him to wait. As he did, he reached for the Copenhagen.

Miguel really wondered about himself. Here he had just delivered the devastating news to these parents that their daughter and son-in-law were dead, and now he calmly sits with tobacco, waiting for hysteria to wash itself away in tears.

Willow and Margery was an old, young couple. Being Willow's second wife, she was ten years younger. She stood eight inches over Willow's five-foot frame. Heavy-set in breast and bottom, Margery waddled where Willow's step sprang from each foot. He had fathered eleven children, seven with Margery. While their features distinguished them as descendants of the Apaches, this was lost as the news of the deaths masked their faces in the lifeless lines of despair. The Pinos now sat in silence on the stone steps of the porch, waiting for Miguel to come to them.

After what passed as respectful moments, Miguel caught the quick motion of Margery's youngest daughter moving toward her mother. She eased Margery off of the front step and into her lap. Willow began patting his wife's face with the coffee from his cold cup. Miguel went to the truck, pulled out the first-aid kit, and laid it next to the daughter. He gave her a small bottle of smelling salts. Margery appeared to have fainted; but just in case of something more serious, Miguel radioed Tilden from his truck.

"Tilden, listen carefully. Down the street from Lodge's house, do you see an ambulance sitting there?" Tilden responded affirmatively. "OK, good. That is where Norman Martinez lives. He is a medical assistant at Twin Rivers' clinic. Go to his house and tell him that Miguel said that he should bring the ambulance over to Margery and Willow Pino's house right away. Also, did Woodson leave to come home yet?" Tilden's response assured Miguel that both the ambulance and Woodson would be on their way. Willow and the daughter helped Margery to sit up. Miguel told them, "As soon as Woodson gets here, together we will tell you what we know. Right now, just rest until he comes."

Willow began to argue that he wanted to know right now. "Where is he?" he demanded, jumping up and down like an elf from a storybook. Miguel simply put up his hand, and leaning over the hood of the Suburban, looked into the distance for the dust from Woodson's truck to appear. After about twenty-five minutes, there it was, about three miles up the road. Both men silently stared the truck right into the yard. Woodson limped over to his mother with tears flowing, more, Miguel thought, from fear than sorrow. Miguel stayed back until everything was again quiet in the family circle on the porch. Then he moved over and took his position on the steps.

"Norman and the ambulance will be here in a little while. I want him to check you over," he said to Margery. She nodded ascent. He told Woodson to start from the beginning and repeat everything that he had seen and what he had done about it. In Woodson's second version of the events, Miguel learned several additional things. Woodson had not been at home last night. Also, Woodson left out the part about the dog, the animal, and Bad Blood. Miguel would challenge Woodson about these differences later. Miguel then gave them the facts of how he entered the house where Lodge and Katy lay dead, apparently from gunshot wounds. Like Tanya, they had no need for any details at this time.

"Woodson, you and I will talk again, later. Don't go anywhere today. Do you understand me? You are to stay at home from now on. Put all of your clothes, including your shoes, into this bag." He tossed him a plastic bag. Miguel leveled these words at Woodson with every ounce of his authority. "Right now, I have to get back. I'll get the clothes later. Don't wash them. Other police officers from Battlefield and probably from Albuquerque will want to speak to you, maybe today, maybe tomorrow, and certainly some day this week. Hear me!" He said it as firmly as he could. His slight command of Navajo brought Woodson's head up with a sneer that started with the curl of his mouth, much like an animal deciding whether it should bark or bite. Woodson's reaction assured Miguel that some level of normalcy had returned. With those final words, Miguel took the old man by the elbow and together they walked back to the Suburban.

"Willow, Woodson could be in great trouble. As you see, he isn't talking straight to you and me." Turning toward the door, he asked, "A few moments ago, I heard a child cry in there. Who was that? Is that Lodge and Katy's baby boy?" The old man answered the question with the affirmative directional motion of his pursed lips towards the window of the house. Simultaneously, he reached out and tapped Miguel's breast pocket in a gentle reminder that Miguel had not offered any tobacco to the *viejo*, the old man. "Keep it," Miguel said as he handed the box to Willow and climbed up into the truck. He looked over at Woodson and asked himself, *Am I leaving someone who just killed two people with a mama and daddy who would never believe it? Such is the Twin Rivers Reservation.*

Miguel had gone about a mile and a half back toward the paved road when the dust from the ambulance appeared. He stopped his vehicle and flipped the switch for the flashing lights on top of his truck. In a moment, the ambulance pulled alongside and stopped. To Miguel's surprise, Weldon Prince, the clinic's PA, the physician assistant, was in the front passenger seat next to Norman Martinez.

Norman's face carried a built-in smile. In contrast, his eyes looked at you from deep, almost inaccessible, caverns. A person's response to Norman always depended upon which feature caught his attention. Norman had come from the Big Navajo Reservation to live with his married sister. Although his ancestry and features were not of Twin Rivers, Norman took charge of the Twin Rivers' healthcare-delivery system, what there was of it.

Miguel had not yet adjusted to the fact that the Twin Rivers Navajo School Board employees were on flextime for the summer months. He said to Prince, "You're about an hour ahead of time this morning." Normally, Miguel would meet Prince's vehicle, and those of Anglo teachers and school administrators, coming into the reservation at the housing project or the Peterson ranch, between seven and seven thirty.

Prince replied, "It is summer time, Miguel. Come on now, what's going on? One county sheriff's van and one state police car are at Lodge's, yellow tape all over hell. Everyone knows that there were shots last night."

Ignoring Prince altogether, Miguel told Norman in Spanish what to expect at the Pinos. He also told him that he should stay available at the clinic the whole day. Katy and Lodge Tom were dead. As far as the *bellacona, the white man* next to him was concerned; keep him in the dark as long as possible. He could be one of our prime suspects. "Let me know how it goes. You will find me at Lodge's." Norman nodded and drove off. Miguel turned off the flashing lights and called Tilden to let him know that he was headed back to the housing project.

Going back to Woodson's conversation with his parents, Miguel again thought about the changes in this latest version of the events. Lodge's baby was at the home of his grand-parents, Willow and Margery, not at his uncle's, Willow Jr.'s. Also, where had Woodson been last night, and why hadn't Woodson mentioned the animal, some would say the skin walker, or the Bad Blood, to his parents? As he drove back on the paved road, Miguel had put these thoughts on the tape recorder. Now reaching down to turn it back on once again, he made a final note: "Find out if it was flextime that brought Prince to the reservation so early."

Miguel had one more quick stop before getting back to the housing project. Milton Tom's place was only a mile off the road. Milton, a great-uncle to Lodge, was the president of the Twin Rivers Navajo School Board, Inc. and the reservation's unofficial chief and "*patron*." Milton not only needed to know what had happened, but he also must call off school before the buses dropped off the kids.

CHAPTER 5

Green Mountain
Monday, 7:00 a.m.

Weldon Prince didn't sulk at the deliberate insults of Miguel Alonzo's ignoring him and the subsequent conversation in Spanish between Martinez and Alonzo. *The power play of my language, my reservation,* had gotten old five years ago when he first came to the Twin Rivers clinic. Besides, in the practice of medicine, pain had its own language. The Navajos always seemed to find the right words when they needed his medical expertise.

Anyway, their secrecy only covered their ignorance as to what might really be happening on the reservation. He had a gut feeling that the events at Lodge's house last night were connected, in some way, to his telephone call to Los Angeles last Friday night. He wondered whether he would have made the call if he knew that his associates were going to take this kind of action? *Doesn't this possibly make me an accessory to murder? God, I hope that I'm wrong about Alquire.*

Man is supposed to be a descendant of the ape. The face of Weldon Prince, however, left that conclusion in doubt. The relationship of his features, their spacing and their protrusion in an outward flow from the back of his head, all gave the impression that Prince's ancestors may have been weasels. Even his mannerisms in speaking and walking begged to be called furtive, regardless of the angle of one's perspective.

Prince had left medical school the same month that his marriage had ended. Easily understandable; his wife had been his sole financial support. In an effort to pull something from the fire of fallen love, he had gotten his certification as a physician assistant and left New York with nothing but a government debt for school tuitions. Luckily, the government also had ways of paying itself back. Working under Indian Health Services on the Indian reservations in the Southwest reduced his debt and, in addition, gave him a reasonable salary. He had no complaints. Besides, his real fortunes now lay with the Mexican doctor. This desert reservation had been good to him.

"What do you think we will find in here?" Martinez inquired as the ambulance slowed to enter the gate at the Pinos' house. The question brought Prince back to the situation at hand.

Prince now let Martinez know how Alonzo had irritated him. With a harsh voice, the man of grudges whispered, "You keep your mouth shut out there with those people. It will make them talk English. I can then fix their problems a lot quicker." Score even.

The three of them, Willow, Margery, and the daughter, were sitting on the porch, nearer the entrance to the Hogan. Woodson sat in the doorway, one leg bent in the normal fashion, his chin resting on it, and the artificial leg, abnormally cast off to one side at an odd angle. Prince, in his arrogance, sat motionless in the slowing cab, staring at the naked scene of poverty and grief, seemingly cast in oneness with the stones on which the family sat. He studied them as if they were artifacts in a museum: the bent heads, the vacant stares, together but alone, caught in the shadow of their Hogan like prisoners to the dark side of life.

The ambulance stopped. Still no one moved. The palpable despair emanating from the Pinos confirmed for Prince that the shootings at Lodge's house meant that Katy must be dead. Why in hell did the Mexicans have to kill her, if they did? Yet, even that possible realization brought no empathy for her family. Rather, in his narcissism, his mind raced back to his last "medical appointment" with Katy. How could a woman so sexually vibrant ever be a child of these two forlorn creatures?

"I want a straight answer, Martinez. Alonzo told you that Lodge is dead, right? Did he also say that Katy is dead?"

"Yes."

Evidently, even Martinez couldn't keep the charade up in the face of the Pino family's desolation. "You check with Woodson over there. OK, here we go." Out they went with medical bags in hand.

As he stood over the three figures, Prince said, "Willow, Margery, Ms. Pino, Martinez and I are very sorry about what has happened. Officer Alonzo told us about the deaths and asked us to check back with you and see how you are doing."

Margery began weeping again and eased over into her daughter's arms, speaking in Navajo. "She feels very faint again," her daughter said. As Prince knelt and reached into his medical bag for the blood-pressure kit, the Navajo mumbling between Woodson and Martinez ceased and Martinez began weaving his way back toward the ambulance. Martinez was pallid, vacant in his stare, unable to get the ambulance door open. *Now, what the hell…*he thought. Prince could not understand how his partner could undergo such a transformation in the mere seconds that had passed.

Woodson hadn't moved. Whatever the slumped figure in the doorway had said to Martinez, his partner was freaked. In order to keep control of everyone and everything, Prince decided to move everyone. This meant he would take Margery and the daughter for a ride, maybe to the Twin Rivers Clinic or perhaps down to the emergency room at the Cuba

Hospital. Prince had to find out if Woodson connected him to the deaths of Lodge and Katy Tom. His paranoia began to rise with the rate of his pulse. Prince knew that he was becoming "unglued." In these circumstances, how could Woodson, that dumb Navajo, know anything about him or Dr. Alquire?

"Willow, help Margery up into the back of the ambulance. Your daughter will go with us. You stay with Woodson." Within five minutes, Prince had checked Margery's blood pressure and had the two women buckled into the seats in the rear of the ambulance.

Prince drove. He thought he would go through the regular summary of medical activity and see if he could get Martinez to respond in like fashion. "The Pino woman will be OK. Her blood pressure is 140 over 86. I want her to stay close for a few hours, just in case. What really has me concerned is her lack of response to the crisis situation. Whatever is going on here, it is more than Katy's death. Now, what about Woodson?"

Silence.

"Talk to me, goddammit."

Martinez had his head down on his knees as if trying to force blood back into his brain. With a trembling voice, he said, "You wouldn't understand Bad Blood, white man. Just get me to my in-laws." His hand reached for the lights and siren. Prince slapped it away.

"Come on, Martinez. This isn't like you. You have seen the worst, here and on the Big Reservation. Did Woodson describe what he saw, how Lodge and Katy died, how bad it was? What's got you tied up?" None of his cajoling could get another word out of Martinez for the rest of the trip. When they drove into his in-laws' place, Martinez jumped out of the ambulance before it came to a complete stop. He fell hard, picked himself up, and staggered into the house.

Within moments, the curtains began to close on every window. Watching this scene unfold reaffirmed Prince's decision to leave the reservation for the time being. The Pinos gave him all the excuse he needed. He turned, checked the women through the rear window, and made the turn towards Cuba.

A state police officer stopped them at the cattle guard at the south boundary of the reservation. Prince and the officer briefly checked his patients. No problems. On his way again, Prince settled back into the seat and began to organize his thoughts. It was just too coincidental. Last Friday night, he'd enjoyed his regular weekend stay at the Royal Inn in Albuquerque. However, the routine of a swim, drinks, and dinner suffered from the complications that Lodge Tom had brought into his life. As soon as he had reached his room that night, Prince phoned Los Angeles to report that somehow Lodge Tom had found one of Dr. Alquire's aluminum cases.

"Roberta," he'd said when his call was picked up, "one of my patients has turned up with a suitcase belonging to the Mexican doctor."

The pause on the other end confirmed the impact of the report. "How do you know?"

"His wife, Katy Tom, told me."

"His name?"

"Lodge Tom."

"What happened to the contents?"

"His wife said that Lodge had dumped them into some water hole on Horse Mountain."

"Be there at the regular time." With that, the phone line went dead.

What a sweetheart that woman, Roberta, could be! Three days later and a thousand miles away, he could still feel the ice in her veins. And it was like this, missing suitcase or not. Did they really arrange the deaths of Lodge and Katy so quickly? Alquire was simply not the type.

Backing the ambulance into the emergency doorway of the hospital, the question would not leave him. "Why did they have to kill Katy?"

Things were slow at the hospital that morning. After checking his patient into the emergency room, he sat in the lounge, picking up his thoughts. What could be so important about a few pills being stolen—important enough to kill two kids? Prince's musings were interrupted by the bang of the waiting room door right next to his ear. Putting himself together quickly, he found his feet and faced Dr. Harris, who was in charge of the emergency room. "Sorry, Dr. Harris. I must have dozed off."

"You guys on the reservation find it all. Margery's daughter tells me that her sister and Lodge Tom were shot to death last night. Were you brought in on that?"

"No, no. Miguel, the policeman up there, asked me to look in on the Pino family. As a matter of fact, there are three or four kinds of police surrounding those deaths right now. As far as I know, the bodies of Lodge and Katy are still in the house. I guess that the police are all waiting for the crime-scene investigators. State police stopped us at the reservation boundary. The possibility of a killer on the loose has everyone held up." Prince started to bring up the Bad Blood killer, but he really didn't know what it meant, except that it created fear in everyone, himself included.

"Yes, I know, Miguel. Mercy, mercy! What those people can do to each other. Look, Margery checks out all right. I gave her some medication. If she takes it, she will stay calm. You take care now, hear?" He slapped Prince on the back as Mrs. Pino and her daughter moved weakly through the door, seemingly resigned to the troubled times back in Twin Rivers.

Prince secured the two ladies in the rear of the ambulance and got on the highway for the trip back to the reservation. He took his time going up into the mountains. He could see a pile of complications ahead of him, but he would take them one at a time. For sure, he would miss Katy's visits to the clinic.

CHAPTER 6

It was now after 7:00 a.m., better than three hours since Woodson Pino woke him up about the Bad Blood at Lodge's house. Miguel pulled off the road and stopped in a shallow ditch. He let his head flop back against the headrest. He felt like a piece of Jell-O; lifeless. Before going on up to Milton's place, he had to close everything down for a moment; stop reacting like a kite in the wind. He was doing his duty, notifying families, trying to alert and protect the community from a potential roving killer, talking to possible suspects, and making a record as he went. Besides, there were good policemen at the crime scene. It was secured. *Anyway,* he thought again, *nobody should go into that house except the crime-scene people. Tilden really came through. I owe him a big one. If I'm lucky, Battlefield's tribal officers should be getting close to Twin Rivers.*

Reassured that his decisions were the correct ones, Miguel called Tilden for a report. Gene Mackey of the state police came back on the response. "Battlefield is still an hour out. We will cover on this end. Cuba County, Saw Tooth, and two state police officers are on the scene. Forensics from the federal lab cannot respond. State crime lab is on the way. We are stopping everyone going in and out of the reservation on the main road. A record of the traffic flow may be helpful."

Where Tilden was a cowboy, Mackey was a super brain, having gone to law school but not graduated. He was the one whom Miguel wanted in charge up at Lodge's. Miguel felt a little better, knowing that the best officers were backing him up.

"Do you have anyone on the north end?"

"Not on the reservation itself, but we have some people on the main road where it comes out on old 44 up on the Tano Reservation."

"Good, good. I'm heading for Milton Tom's," Miguel replied. "Since I cannot reach my boss in Battlefield, it is my call to declare an emergency for the Navajo people on the reservation. I'm telling him that the school should be shut down." Putting the radio back, he continued to sit there for a while, reviewing the people he had talked to and their reactions, trying to tease possible suspects out of what had been said and where they had been. What he had so far was Woodson and a dog story. He wondered if he should even mention it. But he had to. It was on the recorder beside him.

He reached for the transmission lever. His arm felt like lead. It was the same feeling he'd had after investigating an accident that had killed three children who were riding in the back of their dad's pickup. Such a waste of life! With a deep pulling sigh, he drove up onto the road and headed over to the president of the Twin Rivers School Board.

When Miguel pulled into Milton's *ranchito*, Cornell Sussman's station wagon was parked at the fence opening. Miguel presumed that Prince's earlier remarks about employee flextime also explained Sussman's presence on the reservation this early. Milton, the president, and Cornell, the board's executive director, were drinking coffee over the hood of Milton's pickup.

CHAPTER 6

If the Indian and Anglo cultures could choose conflicting images of their representatives, Miguel thought, *they would choose Milton and Cornell.*

Sussman was a longhaired hippie whose relationship with drugs and alcohol was widely known from the barroom brawls of Cuba and Saw Tooth. His natural dirty-blond hair, cut to shoulder length, bordered the stern, square features of a Nordic ancestor's razor-sharp jaw line, now coupled with emaciated cheeks due to a recent divorce, bad diet, and chain smoking. A little less than six feet tall, he constantly stood partially stooped, as if guarding his burning cigarette from the wind.

Milton, on the other hand, wore his status as a Twin Rivers elder and the undeclared chief of the Twin Rivers people with a reserved confidence. His features wrinkled and his cheekbones high, his thick eyebrows canopied deeply set eyes that were constantly squinting due to his nearsightedness.

The two, although totally different in appearance, background, and purpose for being, understood each other completely. From the white man's perspective, they were both dishonest men, but for totally different reasons. Among Twin Rivers Navajo political leaders, dishonesty was a quality needed to make the system work. You took everything you could so you would have something to give to your poverty-ridden patronage. Like their use of alcohol, the duplicity of Twin Rivers politicians was not covered up by suave political machines and paid legal and political consultants. On the contrary, Cornell cut every legal corner he could in order to support his lifestyle, which included a severe drug habit, an ex-wife, three daughters, and a lover. These two men, one the president and the other the executive director of the school board, had been dividing up the spoils, once in the hundreds and now in the thousands of dollars, ever since the board was formed. Their actions, often repeated at other reservation schools, were a tribute to unsupervised federal legislation.

Both men stayed where they were as Miguel's Suburban came to a stop beside them. He slid out of the van and walked over to the truck. "I suppose you've heard of the trouble at Lodge's." They both nodded. "Milton, I want you to call off summer school. There could be some bad people roaming around the reservation."

"We heard that Lodge and Katy are dead," Cornell replied, without addressing Miguel's request or acknowledging the importance of the information he was just given.

Out of respect for Milton, Sussman should have said nothing, just waited. Apparently, Sussman needed a verbal hammer this morning, just to get his attention. "Cornell, don't let those kids off of the buses. In fact, if you are not out of here this minute, I will arrest you for obstruction to the people's safety in an emergency." Miguel never looked at him. He put his foot up on the bumper and stared down at the radiator. His relaxed manner and hunched position belied the sudden tension in the air, but to those who knew him, verified the certainty in his words.

Sussman's humiliation in front of Milton showed as his jerky reaction spilled coffee all over his pants. Hatred for the little Mexican cop glared from his eyes. Without a word, though, he climbed into his vehicle, leaving spinning gravel in his wake.

Miguel let the silence between the two men speak; the longer the pause, the more serious the message to follow. "Woodson Pino was at Lodge's this morning. He came for me. His words to describe what he saw were 'Bad Blood.'" Miguel's deliberate pause before the words, Bad Blood, seemed to suffocate Milton. It was wrong to look directly at the leader. In his peripheral vision, however, Miguel saw him bend over, shaking. Wanting to give him a conventional opening for his response, Miguel continued, "I tell you sincerely, that death scene is nothing like I have ever seen before."

Milton now rested his full weight on the vehicle. Without question, the burden of tribal responsibility, symbolized by Miguel's presence, had suddenly replaced the pride and ease of his patron position. A whole tradition of Indian belief, a Navajo way, for himself as an individual as well for the Twin Rivers people as a community, precariously hung on the words Bad Blood. Could it really be the cause of Lodge and Katy's death? Milton hoped that the Bad Blood message was the raving of a crazy Woodson. Yet, if it was true, he could tell Miguel nothing. Miguel would not understand what had to be done. Milton finally responded with the guttural "oouut," an invitation to continue.

Straightening up to move away from the truck, Miguel said, "According to most people around here, I'm a Mexican, Milton. My words have put a hurt on you. I can see it. I'd take you up there to the crime scene to see for yourself, but I can't do that. Anyway, you probably have your own way of knowing that, too. Now, I can handle the other cops, the ones from the tribe, the county, the state, and the feds. They are gathering like flies on a carcass. But the Indian thing and its effects on the people, I don't want to even know, probably couldn't..." He just stopped, his words hanging out there in mid-air. Nothing more should or could be said.

The intensity of pending events edged their way into Milton's demeanor. He kept repeating the one-syllable Navajo word of recognition that really tells the listener nothing more than, "Yes, I'm here." However, in this instance, Miguel was not certain to whom Milton was listening.

Turning the conversation back to his present duties, Miguel said, "Sussman needed a roughing up, I thought, just to get my message. I have to speak with the other Anglos about getting out of the reservation. Will you send word over there and tell them that I will be at the school in about an hour? I don't think of them as suspects. But for sure, the motive for these deaths could be hung up in them and Lodge's working world at the School Board. Also, I question their safety on the reservation in light of what I've heard about Prince and Katy. Even more to the point of safety could be the Bad Blood effect and how the people look at the Anglos. Agreed?"

What Miguel did not refer to and what topped his list of reasons for meeting with the Anglos, was what connection, if any, did Lodge or Katy have with the Anglos' drug scene?

Milton, still looking at the hood of the truck, nodded in agreement, "At the school, before noon."

CHAPTER 7

Twin Rivers Community School
Later Monday morning

Miguel had come up with a number of principle influences affecting the crime scene, a scene he could now see adorned by five additional police cars and yellow tape billowing in the wind like the remains of some child's Halloween adventure, save for the words, "Crime Scene." By Milton Tom's reaction to Woodson's description of the deaths inside that house, Miguel was convinced that Navajo medicine, good and bad, led all other factors in this case. Not only had the old man been shaken, but the distant look in his eyes conveyed the trauma from a similar event in his past. And that was the damnable part: As a Mexican, Miguel could merely watch and look for whatever would happen. Only the Navajos could deal with the bad medicine.

Next on his mental list of major players came the people at this crime scene, the police from the village, county, state, federal, tribal jurisdictions that overlap the reservation. The differences among them, as revealed by the colors of their uniforms, the choice and makeup of their vehicles, and the various offices to which each reported, guaranteed a dissection of the crime that actually would hinder the possibility of knowing what had actually happened in that house.

The Anglos with whom Lodge worked at the School Board would definitely be part of the investigation. Getting them off the reservation now, however, would reduce the possibility of conflict and backlash from the community hot-heads. But, he asked himself, *what if someone among them was the key to these killings, was actually in that house or tied up in the motive or circumstances leading up to Lodge and Katy's deaths? Would I be setting them free? Warning them to be available should be enough at this time. It is too bad that Sussman doesn't have more sense. Yet, maybe, I can play it in such a way as to use his drug-laden mind.*

By far the greatest faction to be considered was the 2,000 Navajos. Keeping their confidence that the crime was isolated and directed against the individuals killed, and not against the community, would be the real challenge. The feds would be in here soon, wanting to interview people. Somehow or other, these officers would have to see that the prevalent fear among the people gave them a right to rule their own lives at a time like this.

He shouldn't forget himself as a factor. The "Mexican cop" was part of the crime scene as well, and his heritage definitely brought another perspective. His parents had been illegal immigrants in their early days, picking chili in Hatch. His entire family learned to be cautious—and invisible when necessary—in the presence of authority. These habits gave him some unusual investigative approaches and a different relationship with the Navajos.

After giving the state police at the crime scene a brief summary of the past four hours and an understanding of his next move with the Anglos, Miguel raced home to eat something and to change the clothes that he had thrown on earlier this morning. Then it would be on to the school.

As soon as his Suburban entered the yard, his wife put the children and his father-in-law out the back door. The quick shower and clean clothes gave him a second wind. He summarized the events for his wife and laid the foundation for what would be long work hours for the next couple of days. Just seeing him was all that she needed. He left for the school deeply grateful for the strength he found in her presence. Keeping her preacher father at a distance was just one of her kindnesses. Along with the other reservation ministers next Sunday, "Dad" would be preaching the evil of demon rum in the deaths of Lodge and Katy.

True to his word, Milton's truck was in front of the school's administration building. Apparently, everyone had gathered in the boardroom. As he entered, the eleven Anglos, in total silence, found their chairs. Milton's only words were, "Officer Alonzo wants to speak with you."

Miguel went to the back of the room and sat down. He took his time. "I don't like speaking in front of people, so I am not starting now." Chairs began to scrape as though they had not heard him. "Don't turn around; I don't need the whites of your eyes on this occasion. What is needed, though, is that you know a few facts for your own good; and, secondly, that you verify a few facts for me. Number one, Lodge and Katy Tom are dead. But you undoubtedly already knew that. Number two, I am not sure that the killings are finished. So, I want all of you, for your own safety, to leave the reservation after this meeting, whether you live on the reservation or not.

"Just to let you know how serious I am about this, if I see any of you after 1 p.m. this afternoon, you will be put into protective custody and shipped off to the Navajo jail in Battlefield." He let the murmured protests disappear into the tension that he was trying to create. "The state police will check you out of the reservation at their roadblocks. I will then compare that list against my own records of non-Indians who live and work here." He made it appear that he could seal the reservation at will. The exact opposite, however, was the actual truth. At least twenty-five side roads wove in and out of the thirty miles of boundary, making it nearly impossible to lock it down.

"Now, each of you as individuals and this group as an organization had some recent contacts with the dead couple. All I want right now is a listing of those meetings that you might have had with Lodge and/or Katy. Time doesn't allow for individual interviews and in-depth discussions. Just brief statements will give me the general picture that I am looking for," Miguel paused and flipped through several pages of his notebook, simply to emphasize his point with added tension. "Oh, and should something come up later that you should have told me in this meeting and did not, well, it could haunt you, like with obstruction of justice."

Floyd Messenger, the business manager, literally jumped to his feet and spoke far too fast and loudly for the circumstances. "Lodge kept $1,500 from the Board bank account," he bellowed. "He was in last week and said he would keep it until we returned the $60,000 from the sale of his program's firewood and sandstone." He sat down with a thud.

Miguel mentally patted himself on the back. *The tension is working,* he thought. *Floyd cannot control himself. Drugs will do that to you, my man.*

"Floyd, what was Lodge talking about?" This man's loose mouth might open more possibilities and suggest motive for the killings.

Looking at the blank wall in front of him, Floyd laid out the simple fact of possible mismanagement. "The executive director and the board decided that the $60,000 from the firewood and sandstone sales belonged to them and not Lodge's program. He was pissed because he thought that they had split it up. He probably thought that they would do the same thing with the $1,500." Propping his head on his palm, he added. "And shit, he's right. Aw, fuck it."

"Thank you," Miguel said. *He was probably right about the split-up.*

In the hope of rattling the executive director, he turned to him and asked, "Sussman, being on top of all financial matters for this organization, what about the board's loan for the truck?" Little gasps went through the room. It's working; Miguel thought again, his little fishing expedition. "Is it true and how much?" Between Milton and Cornell, everyone then learned that the board and the administration had given Lodge $5,000 from the special savings account for the down payment on his truck. For the moment, Cornell's embarrassment subdued his anger.

Thinking that Lodge may have been pressured to pay back the loan directly to Sussman, Miguel kept probing, "Had you talked to him recently about the loan?"

"No." Sussman squeezed the one-syllable word through his tobacco-stained teeth.

"Was he paying it back directly to you or to any board member?" Maybe Lodge was getting a warning when he was killed.

"No. Lodge told me the same thing that he told Messenger. He felt that we were holding back on his program funds and that he had found a way to get his cut. Lodge's opinions were nothing new," Sussman said.

"Before I continue, I want to know where Weldon Prince is. I know he was on the reservation earlier this morning." Miguel hoped that the quick change in the direction of the inquiry might produce an unguarded response.

Sussman responded, "He had an emergency." The insinuation was that Miguel should have been on top of it.

It did not escape Miguel. "I know that. I sent him to Pinos. If he has left the reservation, the logs at the boundaries will tell me. But to let you know that I know what you know, his relationship with Katy will be dealt with by the feds, who will probably be here tomorrow. Be sure that he gets that word."

Miguel did not pursue any further the bad and perhaps illegal financial management of the School Board and its chief executive officer. Tribal and federal contracting officers were aware of their tactics and did nothing. Everyone realized that this aspect of the board's operation would be visited again by the federal officers who would eventually show up. At this moment, his concern was murder itself. "Now, returning to my original request, can anyone tell of any contacts with either Lodge or Katy?"

"Lodge's kids have been doing well in school." It was the principal, Ben Tate. "I told that to Lodge last week."

"Lodge had his class out on the West Gate Ranch every day last week. One of his students told me that Lodge was still looking for something." This time it was the language arts instructor for the vocational education program who spoke up. "He didn't say what."

"Were the students looking for it, as well?" As he was to learn later, this bit of information was the most significant of anything said during the meeting. At the time, however, it did not dawn on him.

I don't know. Why not ask them?" The woman sounded like a smart ass. But she really wasn't. Miguel knew that.

"I will. Thank you."

After an extended silence, Miguel said one word. "Drugs." The silence was broken only by the nervous tick in Messenger's right leg, which hammered against a table leg. Miguel had long wanted the Anglos to know how he felt about their drug use on the reservation, some of them hiding their habits and their drugs in the isolated workplaces of Twin Rivers. But that would have to wait. "I have already given the state police the names of those in this room who, I think, buy, use, or sell drugs." He continued. "If drugs are found as a factor in the investigation, then these people will be picked up immediately for further questioning."

Messenger, who had previous convictions while under the influence of drugs and alcohol, ran from the room coughing and choking vehemently. "Let him go," Miguel said. "I hope that his reaction is no indication of what the autopsies will tell us."

"School will not take up until next week. Sussman, you and the office staff, including Prince, should be here on Wednesday for interviews by the federal officers. As soon as you come into the reservation, the police will escort you to the conference room in the school. If there is any change in that schedule, the officers will tell you."

"Lastly," Miguel said, "the Navajos of Twin Rivers have some very real problems at this time. Some understand the death of Katy and Lodge as an event tied to their way of life. This is one of the reasons that I am keeping you off of the reservation. Respect the situation and stay out of their way." He raised his eyebrows at Milton, asking with his expression if he had anything to add. With a twist of his lips, Milton conveyed his response. "Nothing." Miguel ended the meeting. "Thank you. That's all."

Within a few minutes, everyone had left but Milton and Miguel. Neither looked at the other. The old trailer that housed the administration moaned in its structural adjustments as the wind shifted directions. Miguel knew that he had come down hard on the Anglos. But it would be nothing compared to what he had in store for Weldon Prince. If Sussman covered for him, both would be arrested.

Slowly, Milton and Miguel left the trailer together, separating outside, each to follow his duties in a culture totally foreign to the other.

CHAPTER 8

Saw Tooth Mountains
South of Twin Rivers
Monday

Grandfather Tom had moved with determination from Tanya's doorstep and Miguel's presence. He went toward the sheep corral. Though his years of daily routine had brought a natural bow to his stature, he now held his head erect over his curved spine, determined to find some answers to the tragedy of his grandson's death. Carrying Tanya's lunch and his old water bottle, he stepped through the open door of his Hogan and picked up his hat and carrying bag from the bench to the right.

Slowly, he turned into the sunlight shining on the earthen floor. His shadow darkened the sparsely furnished room. Over the door hung his old 30-06 rifle. His hesitation and thoughts about pulling it down were, in effect, a momentary prayer. If its sign were there, he would find it, he decided, but he would let others hunt it. Without fear, he walked out into the sunlight.

The boy was standing on the path to the corral. Francis John II was his great-grandson, Francis's boy. The boy took great pride in calling himself Francis John number 2. From a distance of fifteen feet, Francis appeared to be a man with enormous muscles. At three feet, Francis's return gaze confirmed he had a boy's mind. Over the years, Grandfather had cultivated the man/boy's instincts so that, even though mentally challenged, Francis was comfortable in open country. Taking the old man's carrying bag, Francis followed his grandfather to the sheep corral.

"We'll get Lodge's horse this morning." With his grandfather's words, the man/boy beamed with excitement. The horse meant a long ride for him, herding the sheep to the base of Green Mountain. He picked up the horse's bridle and halter rope from the fence. As Grandfather opened the gate for the animals, the goat with the bell hanging from his neck took the lead. Together, they headed for the spring on the north side of the mesa.

It took them twenty minutes. Lodge's horse was across the arroyo and up the side of the mesa, feeding with three other horses.

"Bring him to me, Francis." With that request, Francis opened the bag, gathered part of the corn meal lunch into his hand and walked on toward the horse. It was the boy's idea to bring the tethered goat with its bell. He said the bell told the horse that he was needed to take him and the sheep to Green Mountain. Furthermore, like him and Grandfather, Feather also needed the lunch that the boy now had in his hand.

Grandfather sat down at the edge of a spring. He touched the water in the same fashion as he would a person, laying his hand on it without breaking the surface. His father had built a small concrete retaining tank around the spring. The tiny spot of water still served both the wildlife and the livestock in the area.

Looking after the boy, the old man smiled, thinking how proud Lodge had been of Francis John II. With hand raised, the boy disappeared into the arroyo. After a few minutes, he reappeared on the far side, his hand still raised but now only a few feet from the mare. Feather had watched the boy's entire journey from the vantage point of her hillside stance. Picking up the scent of the cornmeal in the raised hand, Feather walked the short distance to her lunch. The boy snapped on the halter rope and then the bridle. Together with the goat, they walked back to their Grandfather.

With the horse next to him, the old man and the horse drank together from the spring. Like water turning to ice, Grandfather's demeanor became very sober and hard. He knew that nothing from the death scene had touched him. He had carefully avoided touching Miguel, making sure that not even their footsteps had crossed. If death were in the hills around Twin Rivers, he and Feather would find the sign it had left on the earth.

"You now take the sheep back. Afterwards, you tell Tanya that I rode Feather into the hills. She will understand and help you to know why I must do this. You take the sheep for today.

"But, Grandfather..." The boy's face puckered with disappointment.

"Go now," Grandfather said, not sternly, but gently and firmly, while wrapping his arm around the boy's head.

With tears just below the surface, the man/boy pulled the rope and began the walk back to the sheep corral. Grandfather stood beside the horse until his grandson had disappeared below the flagstone ledge. Again, man and horse drank together from the spring. Walking the horse to the sandstone ledge, the old man mounted the mare's bare back and headed west.

Feather instinctively followed the trail around the north end of the mesa, and within the hour, they reached the top with its scrub brush and cactus. Looking down at the vista below him, the old man could see the entire north end of the reservation. Off to his right, Miguel was now heading back to the main road with his flashing red lights. The ambulance that had turned down the same road was slowing to a stop. Farther south were the three mounds of Three Mountain Top. Behind to the west, the mesa stretched to the foothills of the Continental Mountains.

Grandfather's idea was simple. He would check the western and southern boundaries of the reservation. If an evil one who had brought Bad Blood were in the hills, it would seek safety in the mountains to the south and west. As evidenced by the old Hogans and sweat lodges in that region, the people of old also had found safety when it was necessary, whether it was because of soldiers, other Indians, or lack of rain. Men, as well as beasts with bad medicine, were equally wise and would follow the same route. What is more, to the east were the rolling hills and valleys where ranchers had built their headquarters. That way would not be safe.

He rode west until he reached the reservation line. Feather knew the trail leading off the mesa, down to the Rio Pecos. The hard volcanic rock provided sure footing on the narrow turns and uneven grade. At the dry riverbed, the boundary cut west for another three miles to the LaDue ranch, then, straight south toward the high country in the Peterson ranch.

Noontime found him on the southwestern corner of the reservation in the high country of gently waving yellow pine trees. He divided what was left of the corn meal and water between himself and Feather, using his old hat as a bucket for the horse. It had been a strenuous climb to this highest point on the fence line, and both man and horse needed something to eat and drink. As they finished together, he made a mixture of water, soil, and small gravel and placed it on both of their foreheads, praying that the good spirit would lead him and the horse to no harm.

The whole reservation lay before him, as far as his eyes could see, this time looking north. He could see that many cars were at the housing project, the sun reflecting off their hoods and windshields, making many suns. From here, it was easy to see the slope and incline of the reservation land from west to east and to understand the old saying that rain and water never stopped on the reservation, which dropped in elevation from 6,000 feet to 4,000 feet in the distance of four miles.

With the help of a fallen tree and the mare's mane, Grandfather was back on the horse, urging her over the bluff and down into the canyon. He stayed on the reservation side of the fence and well inside the tree line. Since men and animals follow the same mountain trails, he felt very sure that any sign would be found on one of the three paths between Horse Mountain on his right and the reservation housing on his left. If bad Indian medicine were involved in Lodge's death, it would come from Horse Mountain and would return there with the sign of death on it. For his people's sake, he wanted to find no such presence. But this was not to be the case.

As they reached the third and final drainage ditch that started from the east end of Horse Mountain and ran across the reservation all the way back to the Rio Pecos, Feather stopped suddenly and veered quickly to her right and back up into the cedar brush.

The wind was in their faces. What Feather had reacted to could be bear, mountain lion, wolf, or maybe the bad medicine, all of which were either in the arroyo or beyond it. It was now up to the old man to read the sign that had affected the horse. But before dismounting, he let the horse follow the line of pinion for another half a mile. Then he urged her back to the arroyo. In this way, he would know if the signs were in the arroyo or beyond it. But the horse would not leave the tree line. Getting off the horse, he tied her firmly to a tree crotch with the rope halter. To be certain that she would not run off, even if frightened, he hobbled her front feet with a piece of rope from his carrying bag.

He walked almost another mile into the reservation before he cut back down to the arroyo. He did not enter it, but quietly sat down and first peered into the brush on either side. Nothing moved. After repeating this same stalking activity three times within the next hour, he concluded that there was no life in the arroyo. No sign of the snake moving across the surface of the sand, no lizard dragging its belly, no bird tracks. The beetle, the fly, the gnat were not in their place. Cattle tracks were old. Coyote and bobcat tracks had turned away from the dry creek bed the same way that Feather had. The crow and the hawk were in the air, miles away. Death had surely entered the arroyo, and life would not return to it until it was cleansed.

But he must be certain. He followed the arroyo, this time back up toward Horse Mountain. He walked until he came to an area where the arroyo was narrow and deep. Carefully he peered over the side, not wanting to touch the growth of brush coming out of the hollow, needing only to get a clear look at the sand at the bottom. There it was: the pad of the skin walker. The animal's fresh footprint, pad and all, was clearly present in the arroyo, indicating that death from Bad Blood had passed from the reservation up to Horse Mountain during the last twenty-four hours.

There were so many things now to consider. Before leaving the area, Grandfather marked the location with a series of stone configurations easily recognized by the looking eye, unseen by all others. Walking back to the horse, he took a bath, as it were, in the cedar trees. He entered the branches, turning himself around several times, forcing the branches to break and release their sap, and hoping that if he had touched anything of the walking death it would be covered by the scent of the brush. Otherwise, Feather would not take him home.

As he entered the clearing where the mare was tied, she made no movement to lift her head from eating. Loosening her from the hobble, he told her that they would get water at Donkey Springs before heading back up the mountain. It would be late in the night before they ate their supper at North Chapel.

Grandfather Tom was not alone on the mountain as he rode Feather along the fence line toward Tanya and his home. Two other figures were also negotiating the steep ravines and winding arroyos in and out of Horse Mountain. Neither Dan T., nor the skin walker, was yet aware of the other.

Dan T. had learned in the early morning hours, when he was literally backed into his house by Miguel's threatening words that the events in Lodge and Katy's house were born of Bad Blood. Someone had given that description to Miguel but who?

From his kitchen window, Dan T. could see every vehicle coming into the housing project. The front of Lodge's house, however, was not visible. A county police car arrived about a half hour after Miguel had warned him to stay in the house. Then Miguel had left. Next, the ambulance had left from Martinez's house with Martinez and Prince in it. Finally, Woodson's truck had roared down the highway going towards the Chapter House, heading for the reservation's seat of government.

In the meantime, the county deputy had surrounded the house and fences with yellow tape. After that, the deputy went to each house, telling the occupants to stay in their homes until further notice. Dan T. had asked about Lodge and Katy but was told nothing. The state police arrived, more county deputies came, and finally the tribal police from Battlefield showed up. Around 1 p.m., a different county deputy came to the door and told Dan T. that Lodge and Katy were dead. Also, the police were opening the fence and people were to use that opening and stay away from the front of Lodge's house. Weldon Prince brought the ambulance to Martinez's place shortly afterwards. But there was no sign of Martinez. Dan T. had stepped out on his front porch just long enough for Prince to see him holding his knife in front of him, wanting him to know that he knew many dangerous things. A policeman had given Prince a ride back to the clinic at the Chapter House.

Woodson Pino had been the only Indian close to the house for the entire day. After reviewing the events of the day, Dan T. concluded, then, that it was Pino who must have found Lodge and Katy, who went for Miguel, and had given him the Bad Blood description for the deaths. Dan T. prepared his supper, chanting in his mind the song that communicated with Lodge and Katy's spirits. Going back to the window, he decided that he would trust no one but himself in this matter of Bad Blood. He would go into the reservation, towards Horse Mountain, and look for coyote signs in the earth. The animals would know and tell him if Bad Blood had come to the people of Twin Rivers.

Shortly before midnight, and before the moon appeared, Dan T. had left his home, crossed the road in front of Grandma Gonandonegro's, jumped the fence to the housing project, and disappeared in the reservation desert. His senses told him that there was a dead animal somewhere in the housing area. Not giving it the attention that he should, he took a straight line in his jog to a known coyote den, just below Horse Mountain.

The den was in a clever location. Years ago, a twelve-foot dam had been built in the narrows of the arroyo for retaining runoff water for the reservation's cattle. In order to bypass the dam, a road was built into the side of the mountain. The animals' den was at the base of that road, shielding them from predators except those that would pass up the arroyo. This arrangement allowed them ample warning. The only point of observation for the den was thirty feet down the arroyo where it made a sharp bend. He waited for the moonlight to appear. Gradually, the area of the den became visible. To his amazement, the den appeared to have been destroyed. In its place was a gaping hole. He moved along the arroyo until he was even with the dam and looked down to the base of the road.

What Dan T. saw froze him. He realized, perhaps too late, that he had been baited. The two coyotes lay destroyed next to their den. He pulled himself into the sand, expecting an attack from the skin walker at any moment. However, the sentinel of death must have moved from its prey. Dan T. remained frozen. He had to know why he was not dead before moving a muscle. A moment later, the answer came, first in the sound of a horse on the rocky ridge above him, then in the form a lonely rider in the moonlight. The skin walker had run away from the spirit of the man on the horse.

When Dan T. could no longer hear the horse, he jumped down into the arroyo, grabbed the two coyotes, and ran toward the housing project. The farther he got from the mountain, the greater the flood of gratitude in his veins for the spirits surrounding the lonely rider. The safety of his home was within reach. After regaining his breath, he did something he had done hundreds of time before: He started talking to the coyotes. Only this time, he knew that he wasn't talking to the dead animals; rather, he was reaching out to the spirits of the dead animals, and at the same time, he was talking to and taunting the skin walker over on Horse Mountain. He became lost in the frenzy of yelping, mimicking every sound, and filling the night with the coyotes' familiar chatter, surely waking everyone in the housing project just behind him. As he talked, his hands dug a shallow grave for the animals. He heaped rocks on the remains.

Then he sat and waited, as did the people near their open windows in the housing project. The wail of the skin walker in the distance echoed off of Horse Mountain down into the reservation, each cry longer than the preceding one, reaffirming for the residents the presence of the evil spirit in their midst.

CHAPTER 9

Housing Area
Monday

The state medical examiner was Marsh Durbin. He officially declared the death of Lodge Tom and Katy Pino Tom at 10:30 a.m. Monday, July 10. He made out his report looking at the bodies from the kitchen doorway, unwilling to wade through the congealed blood to reach them before the crime-lab people could do their job. The best estimate for their arrival from Santa Fe would be 12:30 or 1 p.m. The Bureau of Indian Affairs asked the state to do the murder-scene investigation. The Federal Bureau of Investigation and the BIA officers would be on site early tomorrow morning to officially begin the needed interviews.

Looking at the death scene from the living room doorway, Marsh saw the 30-06 rifle lying on the floor in the corner of the room, nearest the hallway door, resting about ten feet from the copulating form of the bodies. Miguel had just returned to the housing project following the meeting of Anglos in the board's conference room. He came in through the rear door. This time it was daylight, with air moving through the house from open windows. He walked up next to Marsh and asked him, "What is your first question?"

Not wishing to be offensive to the scene in front of him but at the same time trying to test his own basic intuition, he responded, "Who stacked the bodies like that?"

Miguel had changed clothes, shaved, and was ready to move into the second half of what was proving to be the worst day of his career. On the other hand, Marsh, who had gotten the call in Albuquerque about 6 a.m., had left immediately and still had yesterday's beard. Also, having been on the reservation a time or two, he had left his suit in the closet.

"That's good, Dr. Marsh. That's good. So, you go with a double murder by a third party?" Miguel was thinking of Woodson and the third party he met or thought he had met when he opened the door early this morning. Miguel did not mention this particular visitor to Marsh.

"No, no, no, no," Marsh jumped in. "No. no. I don't say murder or suicide. What I am saying is that somebody and no small somebody, was in here maybe before but definitely after those two people were killed. It could be the same person."

"If that is true, then, he or she, besides being very muscular, must be one bloody mess. But where are the footprints in there? Where do they go out? Nobody can walk on air." Miguel moved around to the other side of Marsh so he could see and point to the gun, "Do you think either Lodge or Katy could have used that gun?"

"To your first question about footprints," Marsh replied, "look, most of the bleeding followed their placement in that position. As to the second observation, Lodge's head is gone, from the bottom up. He killed her and put the gun to his own head, from under his chin. The blast threw him forwards and gun backwards."

Turning to go out the back door, he said to Miguel over his shoulder, "I'll make a bet with you. I say that they just finished making love in the bed. They will find fresh semen on the sheets, and then they got into a fight. He did her in and blew himself away."

"A third party then was on the scene to stack the bodies? You're going with that?" Miguel was just behind him and had to hold up in midair so as not to step on Marsh's heel. It was single file through the junk and tires.

"That's my bet." Marsh responded, turning back towards the house.

"You're on for a buck." Miguel knew that their blasé conversation was nothing more than a dodge from the harsh reality before them. He then took a deep breath just as he had earlier this morning, only this time he had no trouble with his stomach.

"Deal." Marsh left and walked on over to wait with John Tilden for the arrival of the crime lab.

Miguel stopped again near the front porch; and, again, saw a large animal's footprint outlined in blood just outside the screen door. It reassured him that the earlier moments with Woodson were not some crazy dream. He wondered what the Washington boys would think of the Woodson Pino's story.

Miguel stepped into the front hallway. With all of the doors opened, he could now see into the bedroom. The closet behind the foot of the bed caught the direct rays of the sun coming in through the window. It shone a natural spotlight on the emptiness of the closet. A further step in showed him that from the contents of the closet and the dresser drawers were scattered on the floor, much like the back-entrance hallway. For the first time he asked himself who had been looking for what.

He turned out toward the road and let the scene sink in. The residents here called this place the "SHIT" project, "Shoving Indians Into Trouble." From living alone in Hogans built behind hills or hidden in wide arroyos to this, the white man's solution of public housing had left the people without their individuality, without the space to spread out. Junk could be lost behind the pinion trees and the sagebrush surrounding their former homes but not in the barren yards and back porches of the project.

A state police car on the main road was stopping all traffic, backing up trucks and cars for a half mile in both directions. Tilden's truck had blocked off the road into the housing area. Yellow tape now extended around the entire yard of what was once Lodge's house. Residents left their vehicles in an open space down in the shallow ditch. Wires had been cut in the fence so that they could walk from the ditch to their homes. Everyone had his or her head down. There were no neighbors on the front porches, no curtains pulled back, no looking and gazing, no kids in sight, even though Miguel could name fifteen of the twenty or so who lived in the housing project. Woodson was right. There is death and then there is Bad Blood death. The silence of death.

In his memory, Miguel found that ordinary death never scared the Navajo. In this case, however, it was the cause of the death and the smell of death in the air that had disturbed them so deeply. Even his wife had had some strange questions. "Did the blood touch you?" That was one of the reasons why Miguel was wearing fresh clothes. His wife had insisted that he take them off right away so that she could wash them, outside, in water that drained into the ground. She immediately covered the wet area with fresh dirt. As if the answers to the difficult moment were in his snuffbox, he reached for the new box of Copenhagen that he had put in his shirt pocket, remembering again how the withered hands of old man Pino had taken the other one.

Gene Mackey, a newly arrived state police officer, motioned for Miguel to come over to his vehicle. Everything in and out of the reservation was going through his radio. "My guy on the east side of the reservation has just called and said that he has two men and a woman leaving the reservation: a Floyd Messenger, a Cecilia Messenger, and a Weldon Prince. All claim to be employees of the Twin Rivers School Board. They said that they went the long way out rather than using the main road and having to mess with the traffic going by the crime scene. Does this check out as far as you are concerned?"

"It does. You probably remember that Messenger is the guy that killed the old couple. I would ask that you have your officer impress on them that they are to be available at work on Wednesday, especially Prince, so that the federal officers can speak with them." That, thought Miguel, should destroy their sleep tonight. Apparently, Prince had returned from his emergency just in time to go home.

Within about thirty minutes of each other, the captain and a sergeant of the Navajo tribal police from Battlefield and the crew from the state crime-scene lab arrived. After Miguel brought Captain Tsosie up to date with his report and a session with Miguel's tape recorder, Mackey described the situation inside and the need to open the doorways and windows. He made sure to emphasize that a complete report and a set of photos of each area were available. He handed them a roll of film in a labeled envelope.

When the new shift of state police arrived to take over, Tsosie told Miguel to go home. He was to make himself available to the federal investigators over the next four or five days. Battlefield was sending in someone else to take over his regular duties. Miguel watched the work of the lab crew for another hour and then went on home, putting an end to the worst of the worst days.

The crime lab photographer spent almost an hour trying to take in every detail in every room on the inside and every angle on the outside. The animal's footprint and its slide outside the front door fascinated him. He couldn't wait to get these pictures under the microscope. As soon as he completed his work, he left for Albuquerque. These pictures had to be ready before the BIA detective came in from Denver.

The other two men and a woman in the crew decided that in order to reach the bodies, the blood of the victims would have to be vacuumed up. The screen in the vacuum would catch anything big. Back in the lab, all of the blood would have to be screened and tested for any clues. After the first vacuuming, they set up a large fan in the kitchen and tried to evaporate the remaining pockets of blood around the victims. The other two bagged bed sheets and other articles around the bed.

While this was going on, one of them checked the vacuum's screen for its contents: four 30-06 cartridges, three Remingtons, and one Winchester, a small opened pill bottle, five pills, eight beer tabs, four nails, six machine nuts, a pile of popcorn kernels, and a child's small toy fire engine. The items were inventoried, and pictures were taken of everything. The gun was now dry enough to be removed. Its blood-soaked condition made any field examination impossible. It was carefully sacked and stored. All of this took the better part of the afternoon.

Around 8:30 in the evening, the crew decided that the floor was dry enough that the scene could be photographed again before they put on surgical covers and walked across to the bodies making love in death, Lodge with the top of his head gone, and Katy looking widely to the ceiling. Lights were set up from every angle. The regular routine was followed until the crew body-bagged the remains of Lodge and Katy. They were now ready for transport to the medical examiner for autopsies. It was 11:30 p.m., time to load up and head back. Unlike the police, who went home after a new shift arrived, the crew, who had been on the move for nearly twenty hours, was exhausted. They told the state police to call for a body transport at 6 a.m. With that, they headed for a motel in Saw Tooth. Showers were never more welcome.

As the forensic crew left the crime scene at this late hour, an old man on a horse came off the side of a mesa, just ten miles up the road, in the opposite direction of Saw Tooth. He, too, had spent the day at the scene of a crime, albeit a different one, the violation of his land and his people by a skin walker.

A little after sunrise on Tuesday, the crime lab crew was back on the reservation. The bodies were removed and transported to Albuquerque. The crew searched for two hours for the bullets from the four shells. One was assumed to have exited the ceiling and out the roof of the house. The holes were the evidence. A second was removed from the outside wall in the bedroom, buried in a two-by-four. The third and fourth were not found. The bodies, they thought, contained only two bullet wounds. The house was sealed up under their supervision; and they finally left about 9:30 a.m., almost a day and a half after Lodge and Katy met their violent deaths.

CHAPTER 10

North Chapel
Early Tuesday morning

Tanya had dozed, sitting alone near her doorway, back in the shadows cast by the moonlight. She was looking out across the valley floor, waiting for the sound of Feather's footsteps and the return of her grandfather. She had spent the day alone, full of recriminations and guilt. Reflecting the tenseness of her emotions, the sound of a horse's hoofs coming down the trail from the mesa made her jump through the doorway. Within minutes, the horse stopped in front of the moonlit door. Very slowly, Grandfather dropped off the horse's bare back to the ground. He tightly gripped a handful of the horse's mane, steadying himself.

Tanya stepped over and waited for the old man to speak. "Milton must come," is all that he said.

With a voice full of concern for his weariness, she said, "I have food for you. Come. Eat. Rest. I will get Milton tomorrow."

With a deep sigh he pointed to the horse, "Feed and water Feather first while I get the stiffness out of my legs." The soreness simply would not leave his aching hips.

Tanya took the bucket of water from the corner of the house and led the horse over to the back of her pickup, where she had a bale of hay. She took off the bridle and the halter rope and let the horse eat and drink until it was ready to leave. As Tanya turned back to the house, the boy/man appeared from around the corner of Grandfather's Hogan. He moved quietly over to the tailgate, sat, and rubbed the horse's neck as she ate her hay. Francis II's vigil was now over, as well.

When she returned, Grandfather was eating the sandwich, sitting with his head low, his elbows holding the weight of his upper body on his knees. Again, he said, "Tomorrow, bring Milton to me. Very early." He offered no explanation as to what had happened in the mountains.

"What will I tell him?" she asked, wanting to be sure that she correctly heard the urgency in her grandfather's words.

"Just come." He hesitated and then added, "For Lodge and Katy. He will understand."

Wishing that she understood what the meeting would mean, she looked down at her grandfather and replied, "Tomorrow before I go to work I will go out to his house. Will that be soon enough?"

"Yes." There was silence until he finished eating.

Turning her attention to the old man's immediate needs, she asked, "Do you want to sleep here?"

"No, but walk with me to my house. My legs won't get steady." He drank what was left of the water and, leaning heavily on her, he walked with Tanya over to his Hogan. Even in his age and total exhaustion from the day's journey, he was aware of Tanya's loss and broken heart. "Daughter," he whispered, "although you are sad for what has happened, remember the ancient ones are with you. Just go on, go to work. If the People come to you for advice, afraid of events, tell them, like the old days, to look for the light on Horse Mountain, every night, from now on."

Tanya told him the stories that Morgan Tom, a cousin, had told her earlier that morning, when he came with the news of her mother. They were stories about the employees fleeing from the school compound to their homes and about the skin walker in the mountains. Now, aware that not one person had done the traditional thing and come to visit with her in her time of loss, she replied, "Yes, Grandfather, the people suspect something very strange in Lodge and Katy's death. What does the light mean?"

"That is all I can say for now. Only if they act afraid, tell them about the light. Goodnight."

"Grandfather, one more thing. The family meeting for Lodge's burial is tomorrow night, there, in the church. Morgan has notified my mother. She will be there. Will you?"

The old man sighed deeply in the recognition of another suffering woman. "No. Tell my daughter I am sorry for the loss of her son in this terrible death. But I will see no one. Lodge must not be buried until after the light appears on the mountain." He turned into the doorway of his Hogan and closed the door.

Tanya stayed for a moment, grateful in her heart that he was safely out of the mountains, but anxious about the fear in the hearts of the People. Returning to her chair, she resumed her thoughts. *Grandfather, what is happening? You're concerned for the People because of Lodge's death. It should be the other way. The People should be concerned for you and me because of his death. And Lodge! You so wanted him to take your place in the church and with the People. Somehow, you knew that he never would. Is that why he has shared so much of the People's way with me?* Silently weeping, she eventually slept for a while in front of the open door.

❧

Like a gargoyle, the skin walker perched itself on the side of the mesa, overlooking the compound below. It watched as the old man dismounted and eventually retired. Killing him, back in the mountains, would have been easy. But first, it was necessary to find out who he was and why he had gone on his journey. The church and the ceremonial Hogan below gave him the answer. The old man was a minister, and worse, a medicine man. He must not be allowed to meddle in these important matters.

After an hour's search in the brush, the skin walker was ready to visit the old man's compound. It did not follow the trail off the mesa but rather moved through the brush down the side of the mountain. Moments later, its hushed footsteps brought a moon shadow of the wolf man's image across the doorway and a sleeping Tanya. Moving to the ceremonial Hogan, the skin walker tossed a gunnysack and its contents on the roof of the old structure. The dogs in the compound began to growl and move nervously around the housing in the compound. They were picking up the intruder's scent. It quickly disappeared into the night.

The rays of the rising sun opened Tanya's eyelids. She made coffee, Grandfather's breakfast, and prepared herself for work. As she walked to her pickup truck, she never noticed the pad print of the skin walker in the dust outside of her door.

Tanya turned off the road into Milton's lane. Dan T.'s pickup was just leaving. She saw it but her focus was on Milton and the distress that Grandfather wanted her to convey to him. Milton stood by the gate that had rusted off one of its hinges seasons ago. He had waited patiently for any news since his talks yesterday with Miguel. Confident in his position with the People, Milton understood that if investigators found signs that concerned the People, they would bring them to him. Dan T. had told his stories of the white doctor, the coyotes, the lone rider in the night, and the bad medicine on Horse Mountain. Now Tanya must speak.

Milton folded his arms across his chest, a gesture that Tanya interpreted as one of distance and determination and that stopped her short of the familiar, gentle greeting. Offering a nod of reverence instead, she spoke. "Grandfather asks for you to come, right away. Come for Lodge and Katy."

"I shall go. Also, you must listen to Dan T., very soon." Milton took a step towards his house and stopped. "Daughter, it will soon be over. Look for the light." Milton was now resigned to the events that were about to unfold through his hands.

Before she reached the highway, on her way to her work at the Chapter House, Milton's pickup came into her rearview mirror. He followed her until she turned into the compound. He continued on the main road up to North Chapel.

Notwithstanding Milton and Grandfather's reference to a light on the mountain, Tanya harbored feelings of rejection, despair, and hopelessness in every heartbeat. Sitting in front of the Chapter House, she was screaming inside for something to take away the sadness that gripped her life, now, without Lodge. What of the children? Lodge will live in them. With no children of her own, she wanted Lodge and Katy's baby in the worst way. The Pinos, she was sure, would not allow her to have the baby, if for no other reason than the Social Security checks. At the same time, they would not want Lodge's children from his first marriage. They are old enough, eight and fourteen, to choose for themselves where they will live. She sighed deeply, opened the truck door, and slid down to the ground.

Her office was in the back of the Chapter House that had been built with federal money funneled to Twin Rivers through tribal programs. After an hour or so, she went through the motions of putting coffee and water in the electric unit just inside her office door. The percolation had just stopped when Willow Pino Jr. walked in. Somehow, it was always this way. He knew when to walk from the reservation maintenance office into her office and pour the first cup of fresh coffee. Willow Jr. was Woodson and Katy's brother.

Arrogance came easily to the oldest son. It filled his every word. "The bodies were just now taken away to Albuquerque. I saw them carried out. Miguel said that he had no idea how long they would be kept. No matter. We bury Katy. You…" and here the pause was to puff up his importance, "you bury Lodge."

And so the family hatred intensifies, the fighting begins on a new issue. "OK. I hear you. Take your coffee and please leave now."

Nevertheless, he continued, determined to belittle a defenseless Lodge. "I hear that beer and pills were found. Was Lodge on medicine?" The word "medicine" carried an inherent sneer with it.

"I don't know anything about his doctors or what kind of medication Lodge or Katy had. Won't you just go now?" She thought, *Where does Willow get his information?*

"Willow, go, now." It was the unmistakable voice of Dan T. Begay. He had come into the Chapter and now stood in the hallway just outside of Tanya's office door. He was not an imposing figure. Short in stature, prematurely bald on the back of his head. His hairline, however, came very close to his eyebrows. It gave the impression that he was a concrete image, always looking up at you.

When Dan T. spoke, everyone stopped and listened with a definite anxiousness—for any number of reasons. As a young man, Dan T. had suffered a traumatic brain injury as the result of being bucked off a horse that he was breaking. One result was that he now spoke with a strange modulation in his speech pattern. The Twin Rivers people had a fearful respect for him, especially those who, like Willow Jr., had known him before the accident.

This history, coupled with the fact that Dan T. had lived with a Mormon family in Utah from the time he was eight years old until he returned to the reservation at eighteen, placed him at an educational level far beyond the average Twin Rivers' person. Lastly, there was his father, who, although he was from the Lake Navajo Reservation, carried the authority of being the last medicine man to provide the Twin Rivers people with the Blessing Way. So, Dan T. not only talked funny, he used strange English words and possessed Indian medicine. Everyone knew that if a train had not killed his father, Dan T. would today be a powerful medicine man in Twin Rivers.

Willow Jr. did not want to talk to "strange mouth." He left quickly, spilling hot coffee on his left hand as he brushed past Dan T. He continued dancing down the hall, switching the cup back and forth between his shaking, burning hands.

"Thank you," Tanya said, pouring Dan T. a cup of coffee and setting it down next to a chair across from her desk. Finally, remembering that Dan T. was in the vehicle that she'd seen earlier, she asked, "I saw you at Milton Tom's, didn't I?"

"Milton is now very busy, in the matters of our forefathers," Dan T. replied. He said the words with a knowing nod, one that conveyed a certainty about the events of the past few hours.

The silence that followed as they sipped hot coffee was a moment of cultural communication. It passed between them in body language, guttural sounds, the twisting and puckering of lips, the motions of the head in the correct direction.

These signs said, among other things, "I am sorry for your loss. My uncle also died last night. The Mexican is gone."

"I am sorry. But, I am glad that you understand," Tanya replied.

"Do you wish to talk about the death?"

"No."

Finally, her spirit quickening in Dan T.'s presence, Tanya said, "Why are you, Dan T., the first Navajo to express your concern at my loss?"

He responded, "You shall know when your Grandfather tells you." After a pause that changed subjects, he continued. "I just came from the clinic. Nobody came to work today." As he spoke in his halting way, he reached around his back and pulled the knife from its sheath. "I showed this to Weldon Prince yesterday when he returned with the ambulance to Martinez's." After a moment of looking at it, he replaced it, stood up, and, rather oblivious to his surroundings, quietly walked across the room, using the stealthy footsteps of a hunter approaching his deer.

"Dan T., Milton said that you fear the white doctor. I will not ask you at this time to explain it. I do know, however, that, in part, it concerns his contact with Katy. Tell me, are you afraid about what happened to Lodge and Katy?"

Without any reference to his experience last night, Dan T. paid homage to his own father. "My father was a medicine man. He told me some things about the Bad Blood death. Always, it comes because somebody brings it. No. I am not afraid of the Bad Blood deaths of Lodge and Katy. I think maybe the white doctor and the Mexican who stayed at my uncle's bring the skin walker. It is this power that I fear."

"Do others feel as you do?"

"Only a few know about the bad medicine. Some hear the evil spirit in Horse Mountain. The rest think something strange is all. They are now going to their faiths, their churches, their ministers, and their prayers. All of it may help them but it does not reach the evil."

"My grandfather says to you: 'Do not be afraid.'"

The mention of Tanya' grandfather placed a reverence in Dan T.'s bearing. At first, there was a silent stiffness about him, and, then, as though a sedative had entered his body, one muscle at a time unwound and he relaxed. "What further did he say?"

He said, "Look for the light on Horse Mountain."

Dan T. now knew that the lonely rider last night had been Grandfather Tom. He also realized why the skin walker had not pursued him. It had followed the old man, but did not kill him. Slowly, he lowered his head, and with Oriental-type composure from someplace deep in his ancestry, he stepped back and disappeared through the doorway. So quietly did he retreat that Tanya barely heard the latch click on the front door.

Before she could set her coffee down, two men appeared at the door of her office, telling Tanya that they wanted office space for the investigation of Lodge and Katy Tom's deaths. Regaining her composure, she realized that they had entered when Dan T. had left. They identified themselves as federal officers with badges and letters of identification. "I am Officer Ollie MacDonald, Bureau of Indian Affairs, and this is Capt. Clyde Jefferson, Federal Bureau of Investigation. The Battlefield tribal police have told us that Officer Miguel Alonzo will be available to assist us."

Tanya introduced herself as the Chapter's secretary, Tanya Tom. She put the officers in the tribal delegate's office. "If you will excuse me, I'll get Miguel."

CHAPTER 11

North Chapel
Tuesday, 10 a.m.

Grandfather had slept little after laying his aching body into bed early this morning. Going over the events of yesterday, he remembered the many times that he had hunted or driven cattle or herded sheep in the area of the reservation where he had now found the absence of life and the presence of bad medicine. In his judgment, he was certain that the People had a very serious reason to be afraid; the presence of a skin walker. What had Tanya said? "The People all left work yesterday. They are acting strangely. They do expect something is happening to them in the death of Lodge and Katy."

There were many churches in Twin Rivers. Grandfather headed a small congregation at North Chapel. The churches also served as social gathering places for the people. There were singers, bandleaders, choirs, preachers, and those responsible for the cemeteries in each one. Until recently, the churches had offered the only indoor places where people could gather for weddings, political talk, and meetings with government officials.

Fear for the salvation of the soul echoed from every pulpit and was the primary message regardless of the name of the church or its Christian and tribal affiliation. "Listen to Jesus and save your soul. Release your fear and embrace

Jesus. Stand up for Jesus and leave your alcohol to the evil devil." This kind of gospel, Grandfather had found acceptable. But the gospel and the churches and the message of salvation paled before the blood that had now entered the reservation. Jesus may save the Indian's soul, but who would save the Indian? The ways, the beliefs of his grandfather and his grandfather before him, the time long before Jesus came to the reservation, were now the rituals to which Milton and he must turn.

These thoughts moved in and out of Grandfather's consciousness throughout the night until he woke the final time when he heard Tanya's truck move out to the main road across the cattle guard. Already dressed, he picked up his hat and walked outside, relieved himself, and then went for breakfast and coffee at his granddaughter's.

Francis II sat on Tanya's doorstep waiting for him. "Did you bring all of the sheep home yesterday?" Grandfather asked. Knowing that he had or he would have heard about it last night, he told Francis what a fine shepherd he was and asked him to take the sheep out again today. He thanked the boy for his willingness and dependability by simply saying, "Good man," and holding Francis's head close to him for a brief moment.

What would he say to Milton? Would he need convincing? Would he play the political leader? What should they do? Identify the source of the Bad Blood and/or destroy its results? Many years had passed since Milton and Grandfather had met due to Bad Blood on the reservation. The last time, they were a tribe of only 400 people. The killing that time had involved a child. The source of Bad Blood had stupidly identified himself by wearing the boy's baseball cap. According to the boy's aunt, the man with the hat had fallen into a canyon while hunting with Milton.

Shortly before 8 a.m., Milton pulled into the North Chapel yard between Tanya's house and the corral. He watched the man/boy cross the road with the sheep and waited for the old man to appear when he was ready.

Expecting him to be in his own house, Milton was surprised when the Grandfather stood behind him, having come from Tanya's door. They offered each other the traditional salutation but not the cultural greeting. Grandfather would touch no one, except in ceremonial prayer, until Lodge was buried.

Grandfather asked Milton to follow him around Tanya's house and down the path toward the mesa to the oldest Hogan in the compound, one that the original Fred Apache had built many, many years ago. Because everyone in the North Chapel compound used the Hogan for various ceremonies like weddings and Healing Ways, it was cared for and well maintained. Grandfather wanted the people to know that he and Milton were performing traditional ceremonies today, and for this reason, he stopped at his niece's home and asked her to bring fried bread and coffee to the Hogan later in the morning when he and Milton would be finished with their initial rites.

Opening the padlock that held the looping chain in the holes through the door and the jamb, Grandfather and Milton proceeded to the middle of the room under the opening in the roof. There they sat facing each other. They did not speak but looked around at the old logs and straw mud that made up the ceiling of the ancient dwelling. The sandstone wall had been cut from the mesa behind them and carried down to this location more than a century ago. During the silence, both men were taken into the spirits of past leaders who had sat in this very spot and made their decisions affecting the lives of the Twin Rivers Navajo People. Here they had reflected upon the decision, over one hundred years ago, to go to the Apache Tribe for safety, the decision to forever honor the Apache by carrying their names and, later, the decision by other leaders to join the Window Rock Council of the Navajo Nation.

Grandfather, aware that he had no control over the events that would unfold, nevertheless began the proceedings with a steady voice. "Have you spoken to the Pinos?"

"No."

"Then we must tell them that their daughter and my grandson died because of bad blood. They must know that good Navajo medicine, as with our grandfathers, will cut off the source of the bad blood very soon. Navajo police will say a different thing, but I have found the sign of its presence. I now ask you, as in the past, to call upon the spirits for our people."

Milton understood how hatred can raise enmity between families. It is always wrong that the young must suffer the sins of the old ones. But it happens. When it does, as with the deaths of Lodge and Katy, he and Grandfather believed that someone brought the skin walker, the wolf man, to Twin Rivers. Patiently, Milton waited for Grandfather to describe the signs that he had found.

"In the third arroyo out of Horse Mountain, I found no life. It served as the passageway for the skin walker. There is no doubt. The pad of his footprint was there. I have marked it well in the customary way. It is my guess that the walker is camped on the south end of Horse Mountain."

Milton was silent for a long time. "My plan, as in the past, will respond to killings with killing, for the People, and with the help of our forebears. I can no longer be the instrument of death, but I already have in mind the one who will assist us. How he will do it must be up to him. I shall return with Robert this evening and we shall prepare him to enter the Wall of Smoke."

Both prayed, silently, until the niece entered with the bread and coffee. "On your return last night, did you hear the coyotes?" Milton asked, using lightness in his tone. "The same coyote told me this morning that he had seen a lone rider whose presence had saved his life." A smile appeared on the Grandfather's face. Then, contrasting the mood with the spacing of his words, Milton continued, "Dan T. further said that he has fears about the white doctor and the Mexican at his uncle's." Both pondered Dan T's involvement. Milton left in the ensuing silence. The old man stayed until the evening part of the ceremony. He would pray and look for the vision from his forebears.

CHAPTER 12

The Chapter House
Tuesday, 10:30 a.m.

Captain Tsosie from the Battlefield office of the tribal police had assigned Miguel to the federal investigation team last night, when his day finally ended. In this role, Miguel fully realized that he would not be in charge of the investigation, nor be party to its official conclusions; but all the fact-finding on the Twin Rivers Reservation would still be done under his eye. He was an officer of the law. He knew the people as well as any white man did, the language to a degree, and he could recognize some of the cultural undercurrents when they surfaced in the interactions of the people. This morning, as he waited at home for word of their arrival, he wondered how often the detectives had worked on Indian reservations.

Motives for these killings might be found in any one of several perplexing cultural avenues. It could be in the individual memories of a historical chain of events, in the real—or what was accepted as real—acts of personal disgrace on the part of an individual, or an embarrassment at the community level. In a word, the motive could be imbedded deep in the people's profile of life. Being able to find the signposts to this internal heartbeat of the Dineh, the People, he thought, would be the challenge.

Miguel kept searching these cultural ideas as he drove to the Chapter House. Tanya had come to his house a few moments ago with the message that the detectives had arrived. Miguel had missed the officers as they came into the reservation because, after seeing the bodies leave the housing project, he had followed a still shaken Martinez and the ambulance over to Fred Abeyta's place, where Dan T.'s uncle had died.

MacDonald, a seasoned officer from the Bureau of Indian Affairs, was now telling how he had flown into Albuquerque from Denver last night. You could tell that he was relaxed in the sparse surroundings of the reservation chapter house. Miguel was glad to see that his clothing and demeanor reflected a life that had been spent on the margins with Native American culture.

"Miguel," MacDonald asked, "Can you give us your take on the dead bodies?" It was a friendly opening. Miguel noticed that he did not use the word homicide or murder or suicide to describe Monday's events. As part of his response, Miguel pulled from his shirt a five-page handwritten report of what he had seen and done since 4:30 a.m. the previous morning. "This is the best I could do in a short length of time. While you read it, let me set up the tape recorder. Listening to the way I said something may be as helpful as what I said."

After reading the report and listening to the tape, MacDonald, truly impressed with Miguel's capability in taping Woodson, smiled and said, "Miguel, can you give us your take on the dead bodies?"

Miguel recognized the irony behind his repeated question because at no time in the report or on the tape did Miguel give his opinion. But now, he put his intuitions on the table. "Let's see, you gentlemen are asking me if I, as a Mexican Navajo police officer, see the two deaths in the Indian way or the non-Indian way. Do I believe that Woodson, the bad blood mentioned on the tape, and the picture of a bloody animal track have any prime consideration in my perception of the investigation? You want to know whether because of my Navajo wife I may have gone native on you?

"Depending on how I respond, you'll decide if I can be of any use to your investigation. Right?" Miguel said these things as a matter of fact, avoiding defensiveness as much as possible and with just a tinge of lightness. He treated the issues as if they had been dealt with a thousand times before and were merely something to get out of the way, all of which was true.

They both nodded as if they had just checked off the first thing on their lists. "Maybe," MacDonald said. "OK, look Miguel. Clyde and I come into the desert, fresh out of the city. I think you agree that we have to know who we are dealing with before we can learn what we are dealing with."

It was time for Miguel to get the first item checked off his list, as well. "All right. This is my take. Who do you think you are dealing with in the deaths of Lodge Tom and Katy Pino Tom?" Miguel tipped forward on his chair, pausing long enough to emphasize his words. "Those bodies may be on their way to Albuquerque, but right now, their spirits are in the lives of everybody on this reservation. If we do it right, if we listen correctly, we will get to the 'who you are dealing with.' To me, that is the only way you'll get to the other part, to 'what you are dealing with.'" Miguel got up for another cup of coffee, took his time with the cream and sugar, mixed it slowly, all of the time leading them to understand that he wasn't done. He continued. "Forget Woodson, the bad blood thing and even the bloody footprint. That part of it is a Navajo affair and a complete waste of our time to even try to uncover its meaning. But, let me add, I can assure you that the Navajos are handling it. Yes, they are doing the investigating and probably, the judging. Most likely, as we speak they are preparing for the prosecution of it, or whatever it is they do. If we show the least sign of pursuing that aspect of this affair, we will get nothing from the people on the 'who' or the 'what' we are looking for."

"Miguel, in less than thirty seconds, you have given definite parameters for an investigation," Jefferson said. "But what if you are wrong?" Jefferson moved to stand next to him. "You know what I mean by a working hypothesis?" Jefferson, the cub of this team, wanted to give the investigation a different tone. In his ten years in the FBI, he had been on the bureaucratic end of several investigations, on different reservations; but Twin Rivers was his first time in the field on a critical crime. "It's when we agree on an approach or an idea for a period of time and then go out and see what experience will tell us about the approach or the idea.

"So we agree: One, no 'Woodson thing' now. If it shows up, then we will decide that issue later. Two, let's find out what was going on with Lodge and Katy at home, at work, in their families. Let's hear what the people have to say. Three, the lab should give us some preliminary data tomorrow morning on what was going on at the end of their lives. We will use it as we go along." He made an honest effort to keep the authority out of his voice and sought the one-cop-to-another cop attitude. "So, if this is agreeable, let's map out the families with names and priority of interviews."

Miguel gave it time. He gave them the snuff routine, pulling out the snuffbox and proceeding with the ceremony of feeding himself another dose of nicotine. He had no intention of giving them the names and locations of people and seeing them off on their own. "Let me suggest that the interviews should have this order. The families ought to be the last interviewed, out of respect for their loss. Also, it will show that we are careful and have no thought of them being involved in the deaths, even though it appears that one of them, at least, might be a leading suspect. I am referring to Woodson.

"So, the important first step is that the people know that you are here," Miguel said. "I will take care of that in a little while. Also, I would work from the event of the crime and out to the people near the crime." Miguel went to a little chalkboard on the wall behind the desk and drew three circles. "Here is the death in the first circle; the second circle around the first has the housing project; the third, the people living on the road; then the distant relatives and lastly the families. We have to remember that the people will tell us their stories about Lodge and Katy, not whether it is homicide, murder, suicide, or variations thereof."

Without a stop he continued, throwing the chalk back into the tray and dusting his hands. "I did not emphasize this point in my report but the fact that there were no lights on in the house yesterday morning really has me puzzled. Woodson also says, on the tape, that there were no lights when he arrived. Did the killings take place in the dark? Or, does it verify that someone else was in there, at least after the killings? Or, does it mean that Lodge and Katy died in the early evening when there was light?"

Before they could answer, he stood up and said, "How about some lunch?" He knew that there would be total agreement on that point. "I'll be right back."

Miguel opened the door and walked down the hallway to Tanya's office. "Have you met the two federal officers?"

With a long sigh she said, "Yes and no. Today I just want to be Tanya Tom, the Navajo clerk, not Tanya, Lodge's sister."

Through the calmness of his demeanor, Miguel assured her that it would remain that way until later. "Can we get you anything from the trading post?"

Smiling, she declined the offer. Getting up from behind the desk, she walked around and looked Miguel straight in the eye. "Tell me, Miguel, that the children are all right at this moment."

"Yes, Tanya, they are." His gaze was open but official. He turned and left her. The officers followed Miguel out to the van.

At the trading post, the officers remained in the vehicle while he bought a package of baloney, a small jar of Miracle Whip, a head of lettuce, a bottle of chili peppers, a six-pack of coke, potato chips, and three candy bars. About twenty people went in and out of the store while they were there.

Putting the groceries in Jefferson's lap, Miguel said, "Let's have a picnic."

Jefferson asked, "Somehow, I thought that you were going to let the people know that the feds were on the Res?"

"I just did. I mentioned it to Terry, the owner. He is better than a radio. But, also, I did by keeping you in the car. It looks like I'm hiding you. That is the best way for the people to take a good look at you." Miguel drove the sightseers over the newly constructed bridge on the Rio Pecos, a dry riverbed except during the monsoon season in late August and early September. He turned left, just on the other side, and followed the unimproved road that took them up into the Three Mountain Top area. The road climbed for about ten minutes until it leveled off on a small mesa that looked west up the Rio Pecos into the distant Continental Mountains. He drove the Suburban into a grove of pinion trees and took the two officers to the shady side of the slope. He opened the grocery bag, making a blanket for the picnic out of the paper sack.

"The Navajo People call these baloney sandwiches 'Navajo steak.'" Miguel let them get their sandwiches made, Cokes pulled out of the plastic handle, and chips situated in their laps before he asked them, "Did you know that Katy

Pino Tom, Lodge's wife, had another husband who had been killed?" Miguel opened the jar of hot chili peppers.

Both officers shook their heads. MacDonald finally got his mouth empty enough to say, "Somebody will bring the file up from Albuquerque tomorrow." MacDonald's thoughts continued, *"Miguel is smart and his knowledge really puts him in charge of the investigation...for the time being."*

Quietly Miguel added, "It happened right here. You can still see his blood on the sandstone that you are sitting on."

CHAPTER 13

"If you want answers to your pain from Katy's death, come to the North Chapel ceremonial Hogan tonight. Woodson must come, as well. Keep Woodson in the hills for the rest of the day until tonight." The choice of Navajo words that conveyed this message was few in number but filled with compelling threats if not heeded.

These final words of Milton to Willow and Margery Pino left Margery with her head bowed and fearful to her very bones. They were not to speak to the police today. What choice did she have? Of course she would go to North Chapel. Even though she did not believe in Milton's spirits, she feared men like Milton and Grandfather, who did believe their nonsense.

Milton had driven directly to the Pinos from the morning ceremony with Grandfather. As they had with Miguel's van, Margery, Woodson, and Willow waited for Milton's truck to stop by the Hogan. He had spoken to them without greetings, and left them without waiting for an answer. Milton had to show his people a way, not argue or persuade them.

It was already after noon and he needed to make two more stops before returning to the ceremonial Hogan by nighttime. Doubt never entered his mind about the sign that

Grandfather had discovered below Horse Mountain. Lodge's bad blood death, a mark of the skin walker found on the reservation, would be reversed back upon the cause of the evil, but only if they acted in the spirit of their fathers. Furthermore, their actions would rid them of this evil and the possibility of his second or third attack. Moreover, if they were successful, this evil would not happen again for this generation. He was troubled, however, by Katy's death. Grandfather spoke about Lodge as his heir being destroyed by Lodge's enemy. This did not account for Katy's murder. And then, there were Dan T.'s suspicions about Weldon Prince. All of it meant that the people on the reservation sat on the blanket of fear until their forbears, who communicated through the Wall of Smoke, would lift the terror from them.

John Sedillo's settlement nestled on the west side of Tank Road. Five homes were scattered among the pinion and cedar brush overlooking the main road west of it. Robert, John's fourth son and his sixth child from his second wife, lived in the last dwelling, built south of the central corrals in the Sedillo compound. Gloria, his wife, and their two babies were typical of young married couples trying to find housing on a reservation that doubled its population every ten to twelve years. Gratefully, Milton found Robert with his brother, Jaime, shingling the roof of the newly constructed adobe house.

With the men on the roof, it was Gloria who stood by Milton's pickup and greeted him. After a moment of silence, Milton spoke the Navajo words, "the right-handed bow hunter." The Sedillo brothers were known on the reservation and in the Saw Tooth area as the only hunters who successfully killed elk each year with their bows. Jaime shot with a left-handed bow. Gloria returned to her babies, shouting Robert's name as she went into the coolness of her new but unfurnished kitchen.

Robert grunted recognition of her call and started down. Milton waited, trying to think if Robert would understand his need; whether he, in truth, had John Sedillo's traditions. With Robert seated in the pickup next to him, he said, with a gaze fixed out beyond the settlement, "The spirit of your father, John Sedillo, must go hunting tonight for his people. I know that John, for these many years, has no longer been with you. But tonight you will bring his spirit to North Chapel. Come prepared for a three-day bow hunt."

Robert showed no reaction and did not move or shift his wary, silent eyes. He waited for more to be said. His mind wanted to race to the memory of his father. But instead, he listened as Milton paid tribute to his father's hunting spirit, a spirit that was now, somehow, to be found in Robert's abilities.

"Your father has spoken to Grandfather Tom and me this morning. It is you that he calls." The words were more an affirmation of an eternal truth than a source of information.

Robert now wished that he had grasped the significance of the many stories about his father, stories that were more about stalking his game than killing it, stories about the spirit of the quiet hunter. Without looking at him, Milton could feel the coldness in Robert's stare. He was grateful that he did not sense the tenseness of an alerted prey next to him. There was no fear, but rather a confident alertness. Robert spoke calmly. "This has to do with Lodge's death, doesn't it?"

Milton waited and then said simply, "Yes." Both accepted the reply as a declaration of unseen challenges ahead. Milton continued, "It is important that your family know that you leave them in the spirit of your father, John Sedillo, and that is all." Robert spoke the customary end of a Navajo conversation and left the truck. Milton thought, *All things are really simple in the spirit.*

The final step in his preparations for the spirit of John Sedillo would be accomplished in Saw Tooth. Milton found Cornell Sussman at home in the quasi-new subdivision situated up the winding road of Miner's Canyon. Each home was built a little higher than the previous one, offering a higher view of Saw Tooth and the distant plains off to the west. New homes and new people; not necessarily new families, however. They were single people, retired people, solitary people with their own agendas—artists, inventors, and writers. These residents of Saw Tooth were not Cuba County ranchers, nor were they Hispanic, but, rather, a new breed of Anglo in the area.

Cornell could not believe his significant other when she called to him in the backyard and said that Milton Tom was at the front door. Cornell's home stood above a parking area that served three homes. To reach a house, a person had to walk up what Cornell hoped would be a series of terraces in the not-too-distant future.

Something must really be wrong. Cornell's mind stalled at that thought. Milton had never been here before. When his live-in had left and the greetings were exchanged on the front porch, Milton stopped Cornell from going into the house. With a heavy hand on his shoulder, he said, "I want $1,000." The amount didn't surprise Cornell, but the tone of voice did. It was not a request. Milton commanded it. Before Cornell could gather his wits, Milton added, "Do not ask questions. You will hide it, like you and your habits, behind our people."

"All right, Milton, I will be right back."

Cornell took his time getting the board's "special" checkbook and writing a check out for $1,000. Ironically, Sussman thought, Lodge is now getting some of his program money. *But how can I do this and still hold my grip with the board? Surely, other members will find out and every one of them will be camped on my porch for a new loan.* He returned with the check. Without a comment, Milton took the check and departed.

Watching Milton walk back to his truck, Cornell knew that the answer to what had just happened was on the reservation—that part of the reservation that had always eluded him, the cultural structure of the families. The more contact he had about the deaths up there, especially after the meeting with that Mexican cop, Officer Alonzo, the more uncertain he became. He picked up the phone and told Weldon Prince to meet him at Floyd Messenger's house in an hour. Before hanging up, Cornell wanted to be sure that Prince would really show up at the meeting. He said, "Prince, have you heard by now that your fling with Katy is public and that you have an interview with the feds tomorrow?"

CHAPTER 14

Housing Area
Tuesday afternoon

Miguel parked the van in about the same spot that he had early yesterday morning. On the way up to SHIT, the housing project, from their "picnic," Miguel had given officers MacDonald and Jefferson his suspicions about the death of Katy's first husband. First of all, the blood-alcohol level was so high that, in his opinion, he could not have handled a rifle in the fashion needed to shoot himself. Secondly, the amount of alcohol in his stomach and on the truck floor meant that he had been dowsed. That is what the local alcoholics call it when one drunk forces booze down the throat of someone about to pass out. In the time just before a person collapses, they load him up for a good, long journey. It is really an act of kindness toward the one who brought the alcohol. Unfortunately, some die of toxicity.

Lastly, it was Woodson who had brought the news of the death to Miguel, not in the middle of the night as he recently did with Lodge and Katy's deaths, but in the middle of the day. Woodson had been at the scene of his brother-in-law's death, but there was no exact way of telling just when that was.

Trying to put the level of the investigation back into the hands of the white man, Miguel paused for a moment after turning off the ignition. "All right, gentlemen, I am at your service." Getting out and moving around to the front of the van, Miguel nodded toward the house surrounded by police tape. "Going back to my idea at the Chapter House this morning and starting here, there are three or four options. One is to look into the crime scene. Two is to interview Grandma Gonandonegro in that house directly across the street from the front of Lodge's house. She saw me yesterday morning when I came up here with Woodson. Three is Dan T., who lives on the opposite side of Lodge's house, across the street from the back of the house. I spoke to him yesterday as he was coming down his back porch. Lastly, there is Norman Martinez, who lives down the street where that ambulance is parked. I spoke with him yesterday morning on his way to the Pinos."

"Miguel," Jefferson said, "MacDonald and I studied the pictures of the crime scene on our way down here. We even stopped here at the crime scene this morning to introduce ourselves to the state police officer. I've got a suggestion. We read and heard your report. At least we know what you saw. What do you say to the idea that we talk to the people first and then check the crime scene? Just to see if the new order of input might provide us with some fresh insights. This is not to say that you have not done a good job. In fact, what I'm saying is that I trust what you saw and I don't need to go over it again. I want to hear and see through some other eyes and ears at this time."

Miguel took his time, using the snuff pause to make his point. "Fine with me, but let me caution you not to take notes. If you have a hidden recorder, fine. And don't think for a moment that I have not been aware of your recording me all morning." Neither denied it.

They stopped briefly to inform the officer overlooking the crime scene that they would be in the neighborhood. They walked across to Grandma Gonandonegro's residence.

The curtains shook as they stepped up over the curb and turned in towards her door. "That is exactly where she was yesterday morning when I started around Lodge's house toward his back door."

"Wizened" could well describe the deeply set eyes behind Grandma's wrinkled features. All of her teeth were long gone, which brought her dimpled chin almost up to her nose as it appeared around the doorjamb and asked Miguel in Navajo what he wanted. Not waiting for an answer and without any ceremony, she bypassed any thought of an invitation inside.

With a slight limp from the imperfect hip that she was born with, she protruded her lips in the Navajo manner in the direction where she wanted her visitors to sit. She then sat herself on a log stump on the little front stoop, leaning her back against the side of the house. She sighed deeply when she sat, not so much from exertion as from her need to position herself as the one in authority, the elder of this group. The choices for the officers were the steps, the porch, or standing.

Extended families were part of Miguel's life. The Navajos knew of his relatives in Mexico and especially in and around Cuba. In both cultures, the old people had a place of importance and honor. This, in part, explained why the old lady felt secure with the tribal policeman.

Also, Miguel had been through it all before when he'd visited Grandma about one or another of her grandchildren and their problems with the law. He squatted on the floor of the porch with his bent knees forcing his back against the outside wall. MacDonald chose to stand against the four-by-four that supported the stoop's roof. In this position, he was directly in front of the seated woman, allowing him the best chance to record. Jefferson sat on the steps.

Grandma Gonandonegro, without any introduction or question about the visit, immediately began to tell her story in Navajo about what happened, beginning Sunday night right up through to the removal of the bodies. She was totally unmindful of the visitors. Her interest in relating the events rested in the telling. Her hand and arm gestures did not punctuate her expressions but recreated the pictures of what she saw. When Jefferson turned toward him and started to rise, Miguel held up a hand and pointed down with his thumb. Respect called for the listener to allow the speaker to finish her story and then enter her world, not with questions, but with a comment that would have her repeat and/or expand on what he wanted to know.

"So, the shots you heard the first time were very loud." Miguel knew how to lead her back into the retelling of the story.

"Very loud. Outside. Over there. Two shots." She pointed to the back of the house. "Second time. Inside. Not so loud. I come out on porch to hear again. I don't know how many shots."

"Were there lights on the second time that you came out?"

"Yes." Miguel looked over at Jefferson as if to say, "A problem, right?"

Miguel was now translating for the officers. The old lady immediately fell into the rhythm of translation, waiting patiently for the conversation to be put into English.

"You said nothing about Woodson hearing the shots." Miguel needed to verify the time of Woodson's presence at the scene.

"I don't know about him. The first shots sound before I go to bed. The second ones wake me up."

Wanting to let the old lady know that he realized that she saw him get sick yesterday, he said, "It was a terrible smell yesterday, coming out of the house. Woodson probably got sick, too."

"I don't know about him. Clean pants," she smiled as she looked at his face. "The smell was in my house, also."

"Smell was very bad around here." Miguel repeated.

"Bad eyes, bad ears, bad teeth, good nose." She was smiling and pointing to herself. "Maybe you go around and see if a dog dragged a dead animal back there." The tilt of the old woman's head gave Miguel the authority to search her backyard.

He told the two officers to stay where they were as he took a walk to the back and to give the old lady a respectful silence by not trying to speak with her in English. Miguel slid off the porch and, staying as close to the ground as possible, he looked for an animal's track. He could find none. The gentle shifting of the sand naturally had filled in any sign since Sunday night, especially in the breezeway between the houses. *What if I do find what I'm looking for?* he thought. He had come around the corner of the house and looped back another ten feet away from the back door. He started back to the porch in a large circle.

And there it was. A large anthill directly in line with the opening between the two houses had a perfect print of a large dog's foot. Bending over the site, Miguel could see that the elevation of the anthill, as well as the natural covering of small stones that the ants bring to their openings, had kept the drifting sand from filling in the outline of the print. *If that matches the bloody print on the doorstep or if there is any trace of blood on that patch of ground...But would a dog or wolf ever step on an anthill?* That was as far as his thoughts could take him.

Returning to the porch, he resumed his position next to Mrs. Gonandonegro.

"You have no dead animals in the back of your house. Whatever may have been there is all gone." Miguel tried to reassure her with the confidence of his relaxed manner.

"Mrs. Gonandonegro, we appreciate your story about the shots, about your problems with the noise, about Woodson's presence, and about my investigation yesterday." He tried once more to get her to talk about Woodson.

"I don't know anything about him." And then silence. The old lady was telling him that Woodson meant trouble, but not a clue as to the cause of that trouble. She wouldn't even speak his name. Evidently, she had heard him when he told Dan T. about the bad blood. It was time to go.

Jefferson pointed to himself and MacDonald in a gesture of asking if they could speak. Miguel nodded.

"We thank you for your time but could you give us an opinion on what you think happened at Lodge's last night? For example, were there any noises or arguments?"

Miguel knew that such a question would be an insult to the lady's story, indicating to her that she didn't know how to tell her story, especially when a Navajo person never gives an opinion about death. Death must speak for itself, just as living things make their own noise. So, instead of translating the question, Miguel wished her well and advised her that some men would be out back later today to look around a little more for her. The further search was a way of thanking her for her story and for allowing him and his friends to hear it. It also gave him another chance to check the footprint. She shook her head that she understood. Looking at Jefferson, Miguel shook his head, no, that the woman had heard no arguments or fights.

Everyone stood respectfully as the lady rose, steadied herself, and walked back into the house. Jefferson closed the door, and they went down the steps toward the street in silence. Miguel had decided to say nothing about the animal print or mention her attitude toward Woodson until later.

CHAPTER 15

Saw Tooth
Tuesday afternoon

Cornell Sussman and Weldon Prince met each other going into Floyd Messenger's driveway; or rather, Cornell actually had slowed and waited for Prince to arrive. If Prince hadn't come, his plan called for another phone call; and if that did not succeed, he would send his live-in over after him. Cornell needed the meeting with Prince and Messenger but did not want anybody to see them together, if at all possible.

The three School Board employees had to get a few things straight before anyone spoke to the feds. By far the most important issue was Prince and Katy's relationship. Then, there was the point of drug users about whom Miguel had spoken. Sussman smiled at the recollection of how Floyd had reacted to that announcement yesterday. Somehow, we have to calm him down or get rid of him for the next few days.

And where had Prince been yesterday for the meeting with Miguel? The Mexican cop had made a big issue of his absence. They also had to review what Floyd's comments meant at the meeting, the comments about the $1,500. And how did Miguel know about the $5,000 loan for the truck? That had to be jealousy on the part of some other board member. And the issue that threw everything into a whirl was Milton showing up for a grand. What was he doing?

His years on the reservation had taught Cornell how Indians used the disappearing act, and let the Anglos stand out as the bad guys. The "us only" feeling was really accentuated at the faculty meeting when only the Anglos had showed up to find out that there would be no school for the rest of the week. The vanishing act also worked with all of the federal funding agencies when programs were in trouble or failed at the school. The Indian board and the Indian employees were never to blame.

It was always the white administrators who were left holding the bag. Cornell was worried that this same tactic would emerge in the investigation of Lodge and Katy's death. Indians, he thought, loved to point the finger by not pointing the finger. They just left you exposed. Cornell had to make sure that nothing like this happened with the killings.

"You bastards just woke me up. This had better be important." So much for Messenger's welcoming of Sussman and Prince. Messenger's mousy features were emphasized by the wrinkles on the side of his face and the blank, bloodshot eyes with pupils large enough to drive a truck through.

If a room could be any dirtier or unhealthier, it would be difficult to imagine. Beer cans littered every corner. They'd just been thrown there to drain on the floor, leaving sour, sticky spots, each being attacked by an army of ants. Cigarette butts spilled out of several overflowing ashtrays; clothes lay everywhere. It all spoke of Messenger's unrelenting depression. Each of the visitors cleared a seat for himself. Cornell opened two windows, muttering about how the pigpen conditions of Floyd's house matched his drug-blown mind.

Cornell got right to the point. First he castigated Messenger for telling the meeting yesterday about the firewood and sandstone money that the Board were dividing up by taking loans. He next explained what he thought the Navajos might try to do, directly or indirectly. Namely, push the focus of the investigation of Lodge and Katy's deaths onto the Anglos.

For example, Sussman felt that yesterday's meeting with Miguel and his comments about the Anglo contact with Lodge and Katy could be a setup against the non-Indians. It goes like this, Sussman said. Not only were Katy and Lodge the victims, but outsiders should pity the entire community of Twin Rivers Navajos who were enduring this terrible tragedy, probably at the hands of some Anglos.

"All right. Nothing new there, is there? We've all seen it before. So what do we do?" Prince asked. "How do we proceed and protect ourselves?" Prince's strategy aimed to keep Sussman in charge of the issues. In this way, Prince's agenda with the Mexican over the past three years might never surface, keeping his name completely out of the federal investigation.

With his usual foul mouth, Floyd spoke through a tar-studded throat. "Fuck, I can handle any fucking cops. I've done it before. I beat their fucking balls off. All we need is a good lawyer."

"Floyd, shut up, will you? Get up out of that stinking chair and bring us something to drink. Anything closed and cold will do." Cornell issued the command with a disgusted and irritated glance around the room. Bailing Floyd out of his vehicular homicide felony last year may have been a first-class blunder, he thought. MADD was furious with the court ruling of one year of weekends in county jail after Floyd had been found to have an alcohol level of .28 and cocaine in his system. It seemed that the decision to keep him employed through it all could now come back to haunt him. Yet Cornell knew that he had to pay a price for keeping easy control of the financial books at work. Floyd was the price. As bidden, Floyd moved out for some beer.

"All right, Prince. While Messenger is out of here, what were you and Katy really doing?" Sussman had lowered his voice.

"It was nothing more than a feel. After an examination at the clinic, she indicated, in her way, that she wanted a moment of pleasure. So help me, nothing beyond that."

"Do you think that Lodge got wind of it and killed her for it?" Sussman doubted every word out of Prince's mouth.

"Got wind of a rumor, yes? Anything more, how do I know? Unfortunately, there are always rumors about doctors. Now this is the truth. Last week in the clinic, Dan T. let me know that he knows something about Katy and me. I don't think that he does. He's just guessing. But the thing is, the damn people are believing him." Prince did not mention seeing Dan T. standing on his front porch yesterday and slashing his knife in a deathblow.

"Is that the story you are going to give to the feds and to Alonzo? It's pretty fishy, and honestly, I don't believe you." Sussman had to show the police that his office was on top of this thing. "I'll tell them that you are being investigated, internally first. Then, when I have completed my review, I will pass it on to the Indian Health Services for their inquiry. Keep it in the system. Work it up the line. Anything else?"

"Yes. Katy was pregnant. I am sure that the autopsy will show it. I made an appointment for her in Albuquerque. She wanted to terminate it." Prince did not meet Sussman's raging eyes.

Sussman leaped off the couch and stood over Prince, shouting, "You lying son of a bitch." Suddenly it was clear what Miguel was really fishing for yesterday. Cornell's feelings of frustration over how the reservation would play this against all of them pounded at his pride and his need to be in control. "Where in hell were you Sunday night? Are you clear of those killings?"

"I was in Albuquerque for the weekend. Plenty of witnesses. I stayed at the Royal Inn. Usual stuff." Prince remained calm in the face of Sussman's outburst.

"If the feds want to believe Lodge killed her because she had your kid, then it is your ass. You dumb son of a bitch. You dumb, dumb, son of a bitch." He threw himself back on the couch and tried to control the urge to throw a chair at Prince. Finally, he said, "Back to my last thought, I'll tell Alonzo that you are under investigation. But you know that the Indians will never come back to you. And Dan T. will stay on your case."

"Cornell, I am way ahead of you. Don't you think that, since I heard of those deaths, I haven't imagined myself being laid out, dead, some place? That is part of the doctor's risk, rumors with capital letters. That is why I wasn't at any meetings yesterday. I took Margery Pino and her daughter down to the hospital in Cuba, just to get off the reservation. She didn't need to get out of here, I did.

"Also, I can handle all of the problems related to Katy," Prince said. He did wonder about any complications with the Mexican. The possibilities there made him physically shudder, as though the floor literally moved under him. But right now, he had another surprise for Cornell, something that would take his mind off the Katy thing.

Prince was cut off when the outside door in the rear of the house slammed shut and Floyd came in with the reverberating noise, carrying two six-packs of beer. "I had to go out back to the fucking refrigerator in the garage. Hope you appreciate me," he giggled as he plopped back into the center of his filthy domain.

No one said a word while each went through the ritual of opening and downing as much beer as he could in one draw.

Prince was the first to finish. "Sussman, I have one last tale for you. Listen to this. Yesterday morning, Martinez and I went over to Pinos to check out Margery. Miguel had asked us to do it. Martinez goes over to Woodson while I talk to the old couple. Apparently, Woodson tells Martinez something about the deaths of Lodge and Katy. Whatever it was, I thought Martinez was going to die with the heaves right there. Pale, scared and frightened. His pulse rate nearly blew his temples off. He got up into that ambulance and stayed there. He wouldn't go near Margery or her daughter, whom I had put in the rear of the ambulance. He said that I wouldn't understand about some kind of blood killing. Head bent down. On the way to Cuba, I dropped him off at his sister's father-in-law and saw him no more."

The significance of the tale about Martinez was totally lost on Floyd but not on Cornell. To further emphasize the strange activity of the people on the reservation, Sussman told them about Milton's visit in the past hour. He concluded, "Just staying out of their way is all that I can suggest."

Sussman had one more concern. "I don't think that we have any problems with the money things. Messenger, you stay with your story about Lodge's comments and the $1,500. None of it, the loan or anything, can tie us into the deaths. It is his "dead" word against ours. Right? Floyd, there is no other fucking thing going on in the reservation, is there?" Sussman made an attempt to get some kind of assurance from Messenger about any drug trafficking that he might be involved in. The addict came out of his paralysis, jarred by the sarcastic tone in Cornell's voice.

"No. No. I told Miguel everything at the meeting." God! He wished that they would leave. His wife and kids had left him alone; why couldn't these guys?

"One last thing," Sussman said, demonstrating his strained mood by half shouting. "You both know whose ass

Miguel was after when he made his remarks about drugs and the autopsy. It is us, right?" Messenger grabbed the wooden ends of the armrests. Prince had started to get up but dropped back into the chair.

"Now what is that all about?" Prince, not being at the meeting, was totally in the dark.

Sussman told him about Miguel's comment at the meeting, that if drugs were found in the victims' bodies, drug users among the Anglos would be picked up and questioned. "Have either of you been dealing on the reservation?" He wanted each word to be like a hammer on their heads. "God damn it, I hope not." Sussman threw his can and what was left of the beer against the wall, where it came to rest with the others. The slamming door jarred the ants on the way to their new feast.

CHAPTER 16

Saw Tooth
Tuesday Afternoon

Following the meeting at Messenger's, Weldon Prince drove down the winding canyon road to the Sullivan's Everything in Saw Tooth. It was a store of unique characteristics and offered Prince welcome moments of distraction, especially at times just like this.

The interior seemed to have been thrown together in bits and pieces gathered from various stores throughout the area over the last fifty years. For example, three customer booths from the 1950s were just to the left of the front door. Six rows of shoe boxes, about eight feet long and four feet wide, somehow remained upright all the way to the low ceiling, while serving to separate the adjacent "departments." In the middle of the steel structure stood another historical "first." Four plasterboard walls, with a tiny opening to "greet" customers, comprised a combined UPS depot and a United States Post Office.

Behind the mailroom was the main office of the establishment, situated in a square cubbyhole formed by a desk, a filing cabinet, and an unfathomable stack of papers, apparently held together with the same binding quality as the "shoe department." The Sullivan's Everything had an excellent selection of salt and sugar products next to a wall of refrigerated drinks. One of the original soda fountains ever built, with marble top and carbonated dispensers, rounded out the services available in the Everything. Just to make certain that one really did step back a half a century when he entered this store, smoke of the Lucky Strike variety polluted the air, most of which actually had come from Mrs. Sullivan's lungs over the same period of time. Periodic hacks from the seventy-year-old lady guaranteed the quality of the secondhand smoke.

Prince occupied the booth next to the public telephone that hung from a steel beam attached to the sidewall. He knew it would ring in exactly ninety seconds. The final words, "at the regular time" had dripped from the Icicle Lady in L. A. on the previous Friday night. Tuesday at 5 p.m. was the "regular time" referenced in that delightful conversation. Prince picked up the phone on the first ring.

"So, my dear doctor," the first four words told Prince that Dr. Alquire, the Mexican doctor with the German accent, was on the other end. "How have your unusual clinical procedures been progressing at Twin Rivers?"

Was this confirmation that he knew? Jesus! Was the Mexican actually behind the deaths of Lodge and Katy? *Control, control, control* was the brain's message to the deepening heartbeats in Prince's chest. "The patients have died," Prince responded in his best bedside manner. What made him cringe was the fact that he was sure that this information was not news to his listener.

"You say that the two you mentioned in your Friday report are dead. Unfortunate, especially for the good of our cancer project." Still, Prince could not determine if Alquire had ordered the deaths. Alquire thought Arturo must be extremely busy. If he is on the mountain, the natives of Twin Rivers will never again enter their holy realm. It will be a taboo. "One final word, Dr. Prince. Find the container that you speak of, quickly. Our patients are waiting!" The line went dead.

Prince slowly hung up the receiver and sat in silence, wondering and taking stock of his emotions as he would a pulse. He pursued a mental conversation. He had he just been threatened, right? However, Alquire's interest in Katy was not in the conversation. Also right. Did the Mexican know about her? No, at least not yet. He had to admit that he was now frightened by the events surrounding Lodge and Katy's deaths. His mind was hurled into a runaway gallop. Fear had opened the door on the past three years.

"Can I get you something, Dr. Prince? You have not moved for the last five minutes. Everything OK?" He was looking at the wrinkled Irish face of the old proprietor.

"No thank you. Just some bad news. A cousin of mine passed away." He put a dollar on the table for Coke that he never ordered and left the Everything.

The road from Saw Tooth down to Cuba had a remnant of the Old West in it. The ditches had been widened and the state government maintained an original horse and buggy trail out of the mountains all the way to Cuba. Prince, his thoughts wired to the Mexican doctor's words, had wandered to the edge of town, just six blocks from Sullivan's, and now got on the winding wagon trail.

Yes, he was afraid. Prince thought the Mexican doctor had insinuated that he knew what had happened at the Twin Rivers. *Or, did I just hear it because I wanted to?* After all, Alquire had gone to a great deal of trouble to put Arturo up here and to get his cancer medication into the United States. Jesus. Had Alquire actually put Arturo, a medicine man from some Indian tribe in Mexico, out here in the Twin Rivers to kill people, or was it just to scare them? What a quagmire of insanity!

Off to his left, cars headed for Cuba passed Prince without noticing him there, deep in thought. For Prince, it all had started three years ago. Dr. Alquire had approached Weldon Prince during Prince's weekend practice at the clinic in Anthony, New Mexico. Western Health Services had organized New Mexico health-delivery personnel to work weekends at the various clinics for the migrant workers in the towns along the Mexican border. They provided transportation and Prince welcomed the extra money for his alimony payments.

It was in these circumstances that he had met Alquire, just a fellow physician working for the migrants. Within a short time, Alquire had invited Prince to visit the Alquire "clinics" located in Mexicali, Juarez, and Tijuana. Later in the year, when Prince was in Los Angeles visiting his sister, he made arrangements to meet Alquire and, afterwards, accompany him to Mexico. The "clinics" turned out to be health centers for terminal cancer patients, mostly from the United States, and were located in beautifully furnished ranches, one overlooking the Pacific Ocean. Alquire had impressed him with the affluence of his patients and the professionalism of his operation.

In a short time after the visit to Mexico, Prince understood why Dr. Alquire had given him all of that attention.

When Alquire returned to Anthony the following month, he had approached Prince about delivering medications to his cancer patients in the United States. Alquire acknowledged Prince's skepticism and the obvious tactic for smuggling drugs. "You think that I am interested in the cocaine; that I fool you? Am I right?"

"Yes, of course. Now, prove me wrong." Prince had left him standing in the hallway, certain that his suspicion was the end of any future cooperation.

Later in the day, Alquire asked him. "Had you seen any addicts at my clinics?"

"No. On the contrary, I met many individuals dying from cancer, all of whom were satisfied with your assistance and herbal medications. But I need more."

During the week following Alquire's request to bring medication to the United States, Prince had received a phone call at the Twin Rivers Clinic from a Houston doctor. The man had the files of forty cancer patients who, according to him, were alive today because of Alquire. Unfortunately, the pharmaceutical empire in the United States kept Alquire's medication not only off the shelves, but out of the country. "Help him if you can," was the final request from the Houston doctor. A later phone call to the American Medical Association in Texas had verified the Houston man's certification.

And help him Prince did, beginning after his second visit to Alquire's Juarez clinic, where he encountered more suffering Americans. From that point on, quite openly, once a month, in a new leather bag provided by Alquire, Prince had brought an aluminum case of the doctor's medication to the Twin Rivers Reservation. There, on his monthly visit to an old Navajo man named Fred Abeyta, Prince would leave the aluminum case in Mr. Abeyta's Hogan. From there, Fred's new caretaker, Arturo, an Indian associate of Dr. Alquire from Mexico, took the medication and, somehow, after storing it on Horse Mountain, entered it into Alquire's distribution system. Prince had been reimbursed generously for his efforts.

Now reflecting, Prince realized why Martinez had gone into his stupor. Most Indians believed in the interaction of spirits. Twin Rivers is a house of fear right now because of the evil spirit that Arturo brought to Horse Mountain. It is just preposterous, but there it is. He was coming to the conclusion that he should take his story to the police. But to which ones: tribal, state, county, or federal? None that he knew would believe it.

But still the question: *Did Arturo kill the Navajos and thereby stupidly draw law enforcement's attention to Alquire's little operation? That simply makes no sense. What don't I know?*

CHAPTER 17

It had been a busy morning. Dan T. had just returned from the family meeting over his uncle's death, his visit with Milton Tom, and, later in the morning, his few moments with Tanya at the Chapter House.

The old 1972 Chevy truck still hauled him about. Dan T. was proud of the truck for several reasons. From bumper to bumper, it was totally rebuilt. Moreover, he had done it with used parts, the exception, of course, being the engine parts, which cost him $475. The paint job had the finish of sandpaper, but who at Twin Rivers lived in a dust-free environment?

The police were now allowing housing residents to drive by the crime scene instead of parking off the road as they did on Monday. Dan T. had naturally noticed Miguel's van when he turned off the highway and, of course, he saw the three men visiting Grandma Gonandonegro. All had taken note, he was sure, of his return, as well.

It was no surprise, then, when the three officers knocked on his back door and wanted to speak with him. For all of the unusual habits attributed to his blow on the head, Dan T. had accepted some of the white man's social graces, which now accounted for the fact that the officers were seated around the kitchen table, waiting for the coffee to be served. Dan thought that a little camp-style coffee, brought to a boil in an open pot and then left to settle, would clear their heads of any weariness. Clean cups on the Formica table, sugar, and a can of pasteurized milk lay waiting for the liquid refreshment. Each man accepted his portion dipped right out of the steaming pot and quickly set on the table. Dan T. sat on the kitchen counter because there were only three chairs to his kitchen ensemble.

After the cultural encounter with the old lady, the two detectives warmed to the white man's amenities in Dan T.'s hospitality. Miguel loved the contradictions seemingly built into Dan T.'s personality. As previously agreed, the two agents had the opportunity to display their investigative prowess with the English-speaking Navajo. Miguel sat quietly.

After the introductions, Dan T. wanted them to know that he knew what they wanted to know. He laughed to himself as he began. "Let me save you a lot of trouble, OK? There were four shots, two on two different occasions. The last set occurred early Monday morning. The first set was Lodge shooting into the air out there in the back of his house. I didn't see the shots out there, but I saw Lodge turn and go back into the house, laughing like hell."

"Are you sure about the number of shots?" Jefferson loved the pace of this conversation.

"Yes. Well, maybe there was more than two shots the second time. Maybe the first one didn't wake me up. But only one after I heard the first one Lodge shot outside." Dan T. left all of his options open.

"Did he appear drunk when you saw him the first time?" MacDonald asked.

"No. But I really couldn't tell." Dan T. no longer addressed his questioners, only the questions. He walked over to the back-door window, pulled back the curtain, and talked as though he were looking at the scene.

"Did you see Katy?"

"No." After a moment's hesitation, he added. "But she was within earshot because Lodge kept talking to the back door."

"What kind of clothes did Lodge have on?" Jefferson wanted to get as much of the scene as possible.

After a pause and a further shifting of the curtains, Dan T said, "Shorts, under shorts."

"You say that Lodge was talking to Katy, although you didn't see her. Did they seem to be arguing?"

Dan T. leaned forward and put his ear to the window, as though he were listening, "No, none that I heard."

"Did you notice any visitors during the night?" Mac-Donald moved the conversation forward.

Again, Dan T. moved, looking for someone. "None that I saw."

"Do you have any thoughts on what might have happened that caused the last shots in the house?" Jefferson asked.

Assuming his former position on the counter, Dan T. answered. "No."

"So you heard nothing more and saw nothing more after Lodge went into the house. Right?" Jefferson held up his hand to let everyone know that he wasn't finished. "About Woodson. When was the first time you saw him?"

"I never saw him," Dan T. said. It was fun to take these guys down some blind paths.

"But he was with Miguel yesterday morning," Jefferson said. "How could you have missed him?" *I just caught the little shit in a lie,* he thought.

"OK. Woodson was with Miguel. If you say so. Maybe. But I cannot see the front of the house from here. Look for yourself."

Jefferson did. After reseating himself, he continued. "Let me come back to that. Miguel says in his report that he told you to get back in the house. Why were you standing at the door, dressed, when he came around the house?"

Dan T. replied, "Don't you get up before the sun, Officer? I heard the vehicles come across the cattle guard and I could see the lights stop in front of Lodge's house."

"Why did Miguel use the words, 'Bad Blood?'"

Miguel thought that Dan T. would stop them right there. But he didn't. Without any hesitation, Dan T. answered, "Deaths in 'bad blood' are often when relatives of the Indian are involved."

"Does that mean that someone who is related to them killed Lodge and Katy?" Jefferson didn't look at Miguel, but both knew that Jefferson was testing Miguel's theory on Dan T.

"Definitely not, White Man. Definitely not." Before his inquirers could follow with another question, Dan T. asked, "Did anybody talk about the cries of the coyote last night?"

Miguel did not register a reaction but the two detectives picked up on it. "Tell us what you are talking about, Dan T."

"The other night, I heard the cries of the coyotes." Dan T.'s eyes looked at each of his visitors with anticipation that he might have added something to their investigation. Besides, Dan T. really wanted to know if Grandma had mentioned his activity from Monday night.

Unaware of Dan T.'s excursion, Miguel thought, *Bullshit. Dan T. is putting out a false trail for the white boys.*

Surprisingly, MacDonald followed up and showed a little savvy on the coyote thing by saying, "I remember coyotes crying when I camped with my family during the hunting season. I am never ready for them. They always alarm us. Why do you mention it? Something to do with Lodge's death?"

"Nothing in particular. I thought that others might have heard." When his knowledge of the coyote made no impression on the detectives, Dan T. proceeded to tell them a coyote story about two men in search of a deer.

Miguel thought he would just put an end to Dan T.'s "up the road with you tale" and interject a little surprise of his own. "Dan T.," he said. "A couple of things. First, I'm sorry about the death of your uncle. As you probably know, your cousin came and got me early that morning." With a nod, Dan T. recognized the sympathy. "A second thing. Dan T., was there a light on in the house when you heard the second group of shots?"

"Yes."

"That means that you got up, right?" Miguel continued.

"Yes. I sat right where you are for a while, listening."

"Lastly, what did you and Milton have to say to each other this morning?" Miguel shifted languages and asked in Navajo. The suspense of all three now hung in the air. Miguel's tone, in Navajo, told Dan T. to consider before he answered. Miguel followed up in English. "Is Milton feeling better? He did not look too good yesterday morning when I told him to close the school." Miguel skirted the real question of the bad blood. But in referring to Milton, he let Dan T. know that whatever the community was doing about the deaths, at least Miguel was aware and would be watching.

"You know that the Mexican is gone?" Dan T. hesitated just long enough to see if Miguel had any reaction to the mention of the Mexican. If so, he wanted Miguel to understand that he, too, had followed the events at Fred Abeyta's. Apparently, though, Miguel knew nothing about Weldon Prince's monthly visit to his uncle or the aluminum cases that he left there. When he saw no reaction in Miguel, Dan T. continued, "Milton is fine. He told me about leaving school out until next week. This will give everybody a chance to attend to their family obligations for the Pinos and the Toms."

Miguel's questions and conversation had effectively ended the interview for MacDonald and Jefferson. The coyote thing wasn't going anywhere. But each of the detectives had more than one question for Miguel as soon they got him alone. They pushed back their chairs and stood up.

Dan T. felt that he had to have the last surprise in his little game with Miguel . The detectives were out of this foray. He walked the trio to the back door, asking himself if he should give Miguel Prince's Mexican or Prince's girl to Miguel. As Miguel crossed in front of him, Dan T. said in Navajo, "Mr. Prince will know something about Katy." Dan T. would save the Mexican until later. The door closed.

"What did he say, Miguel ?" The impatient and jumpy tone in Jefferson's question clearly indicated that the caffeine in Dan T.'s "camp-coffee-from-hell" had reached his brain.

"Dan T. said that we should talk to Prince real soon because he knows something about Katy."

"Well, let's turn around and find out right now what that information might be." MacDonald was on his way back up the porch steps.

"No use. Dan T. has just given us his parting gift."

"I feel like a torpedo ready to go off," Jefferson conceded on the way back to the van. The potency of Dan T.'s coffee bordered on the European espresso, and he had drunk an entire cup. Apparently, MacDonald's robust frame could absorb the caffeine. He knew now why Miguel had only sipped and wasted the coffee.

In addition to the caffeine rush, Jefferson also felt that they had to debrief these two interviews before going on any more questioning expeditions. Also, on the way over to Pino's, Miguel had promised to go into the reasons for his disappearance at the old lady's house. Finally, Dan T. had created more than his share of new leads with the Prince comments.

"Miguel, let's sit down and talk," suggested MacDonald, knowing that his ability to catalogue any information from the interviews was disappearing with each new idea or input.

"I promise to stay with you guys until you're satisfied with every detail. But before we digest anything, I think you should look over the crime scene." Miguel wanted the bloody footprint in their minds before talking about his find at the Gonandonegros'.

Jefferson raised his hand to protest and would have loved to verbally rip into this little squirt of an Indian-loving cop but, instead, took his cue from MacDonald's frown. They quickly walked around to the front of Lodge's house. Approaching the house, they spoke briefly with the state police officer and listened to his activity report of the day. The two detectives then followed Miguel to the front steps, where he dropped to his haunches and pointed to the blood-red footprint of one very large dog; the animal mentioned in Miguel's report.

"Imagine, if you will, a large letter V," Miguel began. He drew one with his finger in the dust on the porch. "At the bottom of the V are the deaths of the two young people in this house. The print that you are looking at is the first step in the Navajo way of understanding and making sense out of this crime. It is the beginning of this side of the V. The other side of the V is the non-Indian investigation part, the part for you, the cop over there, and the people that we have talked to today.

"So what I am trying to say is this. For a while, you have to store your information about this crime in two very tight compartments. Both sides of the V come out of this house but are going in different directions. One goes off into that mountain up there. The other, I don't know just yet. Sooner or later, though, they will turn back to each other. You will see it happen," and here he paused in order to emphasize the point, "if you don't jump to early conclusions."

Jefferson wasn't buying into Miguel's analysis. For the time being he would not respond directly to Miguel's explanation, but by turning his attention to the animal's print, he thought that he could tell Miguel in a nice way that he didn't buy it. "What if that 'print' is not a print but a quirky look-alike that came from the dirt of Woodson's boot after he had stepped in the blood inside the house? You did say in your report that he had blood on him."

Miguel ignored the bait. Taking his time rising, he turned and walked down the steps. He took out the snuffbox and as if he were addressing it, said, "What if I were to tell you that I found a print just like that in an anthill over behind Grandma's house? That is what I meant about something going to the mountain." Neither detective felt an opening for a comment because the information apparently belonged to the snuff ritual. Until Miguel finished putting it into his lower lip, they had to wait.

"Right now, I am figuring on how to compare the two prints…are you listening?…without raising any suspicion in the community that we are interested in the Navajo direction of this crime. I have to prove, or disprove, the likeness of these two prints simply to keep us out of the Navajo side. Otherwise, as I add it up, there is not a chance in hell that we will understand Lodge and Katy's deaths from our side of the equation. *Comprende?*"

"You mean that the only way to keep our investigation objective is to acknowledge what is and what is not ours to investigate?" MacDonald spoke slowly.

"Something like that." Miguel could see him coming around to the possibility that there might be a new presence in this case. Jefferson, on the other hand, was another story. His disapproval was quite evident in his silence. Miguel moved on. "If we can prove that these prints came from the same animal, it is the Indian side of things; and we can forget it. But if it is a boot, like you said, then it belongs to us."

MacDonald now knew that any help from Jefferson at this time was out of the question. Letting Miguel have the lead once again, he asked. "What do you have in mind?"

"I am going to get the state policeman's camera. It's a lot better than mine. I promised Grandma Gonandonegro that I would get some people and check around her house for any dead animals that might have caused her trouble last night. Do you see those two boys on the driveway down there? They are the Garcia kids. While you look around inside, they will help me search in the bushes in back of Grandma's house. I'll get the pictures without anybody knowing what's happening and be back in thirty minutes."

They agreed. The Garcia boys came running up to Miguel when his whistle got their attention. After telling them what he wanted, he sent them in several sweeps of the area. On the pretense of looking into the brush next to the fence line that divided the property, Miguel got his pictures. He instructed one of the boys to go to Grandma and tell her that everything was clear around her house. She should have no fears.

Returning to Lodge's house, Miguel finished the role of film by taking pictures of the print on the porch. He removed the film and handed it to MacDonald as they exited the front door. "Have your lab boys verify or deny likenesses."

CHAPTER 18

Tanya awoke with a start from the loud knock at her front door. Rolling over, she threw her legs over the side of the bed, paused to collect herself from a deep sleep, and hurried out to see who it was.

"You will come to Grandfather's tonight, to the ceremonial Hogan. After the Pinos leave us, I will come for you." With those words, Milton Tom turned and left. She watched as his truck slowly moved towards the ceremonial Hogan. No opportunity for a reply; not an order but just a simple statement that she was to join the ceremony later tonight.

Tanya closed the door, stood there looking at the basket of fried bread on the table, and was relieved that she had an hour before the relatives' meeting at six o'clock. As she had told Grandfather before leaving in the morning, the relatives were meeting this evening to make funeral arrangements for Lodge.

She had left the Chapter House around two o'clock, sometime after Miguel had departed with the police officers. When she was finally alone, she had written a letter to the Navajo District Court asking for the custody of Lodge's children. When she arrived home, she immediately checked on her grandfather, only to find his Hogan empty. His ceremonial bag was missing from its nail near the cupboard. This meant only one thing; he was at the ceremonial Hogan and would need food.

Making the fried bread had taken her about an hour. After leaving some of the bread and water outside of the Hogan of prayer, she had lain down for a moment. It was now two hours later. But she did feel better and knew that she was now ready for events of the evening. She reheated the coffee that she made when she came home from work. Strange, the day had started out with her driving to Milton's home and asking him to come to her Grandfather. Now, here he was, near the end of the day, telling her to come to Grandfather this evening.

Looking out the window with the coffee offering its warmth of fragrance and steam, she saw the pickups begin to gather at the North Chapel. As was the custom, they were forming a circle around the entrance to the front door of the church. Like the chairs in the church, parking spaces were occupied, it seemed, in deference to the women's position in the ceremony that was to take place. The space right in front of the door should be left for the vehicle with her mother in it. When she saw that space filled, she knew it would be time to go.

Throughout the day, she had found herself praying for Lodge, his family, and herself. How intensely she felt the need for someone or something outside of herself to give some explanation for what had happened. This grasping rose up from within to a point that it almost choked her. *It could have been different, Lodge*, she thought. *But we had no power to make it different. God, how long we were separated? Dumped by our mother on relatives who took us for a few dollars. They never wanted us, always putting us last among the other children in the family. I cannot remember seeing you until I was five years old, and my auntie told me that you were my brother. I could not believe it. If we were brother and sister, why were we not together? I wanted to be with you so badly. You were all that mattered. I just lived through those horrible days for two reasons. I wanted to see you again and to be with the kind old man whom I later learned to love so much, our grandfather. How many times I was told that my Navajo family should be enough for me. Am I to blame that it wasn't?*

Tanya brought her reverie to a close with a determination to revisit those early years at a more peaceful time. Now, duty to her mother called—a mother whom she had never learned to love or, in fact, had ever experienced as a mother. She laid her cup in the sink, took her coat from the peg beside the window, put the basket filled with fried bread and a pound of coffee on her arm, and walked out toward the church. The distance from her door to the church was maybe a hundred yards, a distance that she had covered with the joy of new births, weddings, and fiestas, and, now, once again, with the sadness of death. This evening in the fading daylight, however, each step to the church increased the certainty of Lodge's separation in her aching heart. The wrenching within seemed so tied to the rhythm of her step that she actually stopped and took a deep breath. It did not go away.

The women from Grandfather's family were well represented. She could tell, from the trucks, which ones were actually inside. The men, as was the custom, were outside in the trucks and would never have come by themselves. She caught no one's gaze but kept her eyes down and walked rigidly up the steps of the little church, noting that the parking place for her mother's pickup was empty. As she was about to reach for the door, the auntie who had raised her opened it for her; a cousin took the basket, and Tanya was escorted to a chair in the back of the church.

Already, the central group in the big circle at the front under the powerful lights was discussing the possible times for the memorial service. It was a service that would follow sometime after the burial and would be a family tribute to Lodge. To the left, in a smaller circle, were Lodge's in-laws, two of Katy's sisters and a sister of Katy's mother. They did not have a say in the decisions concerning Lodge and were perfectly still. To the right side was no one. Empty chairs designated the place where the women from Lodge's father's side would have gathered. Their progeny, as in life, remained unrecognized in death.

"Tanya, do you have any idea when Lodge's body will be released for burial?" It was her auntie.

"No, I do not. Miguel said that the best he could estimate is that it would be early next week."

"I guessed as much. I believe that planning the burial for a week from tomorrow would be as close as we can make it. By the weekend, we should know something definite. Will Katy be buried with Lodge?"

"I can tell you that the Pinos will definitely not allow Katy to be buried with Lodge. Already, Willow Jr. has told me that much. He came to my office in the Chapter House and informed me that they want nothing to do with Lodge. They believe that he killed Katy." The delegation from Katy's family nodded their heads in agreement. The bitterness began to flood her words, so she stopped and asked, "Is it true that the Pinos have the children?"

"Yes, they have the baby. Lodge's older ones are in Saw Tooth with their mother," the aunt said. The women in the small circle to the left, the Pino women, again confirmed everything with grunts of affirmation.

Her heart ached, knowing that Lodge's youngest child, Lodge Tom Jr., would become, in fact, a Pino. Yes, the name of Lodge Tom would live on in his son, but the Tom spirit would now be absent in him. She would fight for him in the courts, knowing that her chances were zero because she had no husband. And, of course, because she was only half

Navajo, the courts would believe that the baby would not be raised to appreciate his culture. How far from the truth that belief really was. Grandfather had seen to that with his love and willingness to give her all of his medicines before he would pass to the spirits. It was one of these ancient Navajo beliefs that she was now about to call upon.

Perhaps it was being the last living child in her immediate family that gave her the courage to take her stand and protect the family name of her mother. Standing up in her place in the back of the church, she raised her voice. "It is now apparent that my mother will not be here this evening. I am sorry for that." The conversations throughout the church hushed. "I have no intention of coming forth and sitting in my mother's chair. Yet, I tell you now that I am, from this moment, the traditional head of my family. Lodge shall be buried with the mother's wail and I shall lead it."

No one stood to protest her words. No one moved to show disapproval. She continued. "Some will say that a half-breed woman has no right in the Navajo way. To them, I say that my Grandfather has given me that right. I believe that I was brought to this reservation by the spirits of my forefathers for a purpose which, at this moment, begins to take shape." Tanya knew that her exact words would be repeated in every house on the reservation in the next couple of days. People did it because they wanted to hear how the words sounded to others and how others reacted to them.

"Throughout my life, I have not been accepted in the cultural place of a Navajo woman," she paused long enough to stress the fact, "by any of you. But my grandfather has accepted me. His acceptance has been enough for me and for the spirits of our people." The mood began to rise within the church even though not a soul shifted in her chair. Tension within the women showed itself in the angle and turn of the head so that the ear might hear more clearly. The eyes of every person, as though linked together, centered in unison on the little woman standing in the shadows of the single light hanging from the center of the roof.

"I do not hold anything against the Twin Rivers customs which you have not shared with me. But know this. The spirits of our people reach farther and wider than the customs practiced by you." Still no movement. Tanya felt that the spirits were, indeed, present to her. "Please know that I will bury my brother on a time and date that I will give the community. The burial will be private for my family only. Your donations, jewelry, and tribal assistance will not be necessary. At a later time, a memorial service shall take place to which all of the community will be invited. For this, too, I will give the time and date to the community. Let it be known that I have spoken."

Tanya then turned and walked over to her auntie. "Please provide everyone with something to eat," pointing to the bread and coffee. "Thank you. Good night." It had been a short but historical meeting.

CHAPTER 19

North Chapel
Tuesday evening

G randfather had fallen asleep in the early afternoon on
the Hogan's Navajo rugs, shortly after Milton had left.
He awoke, now, as he had so many times in his life, lying on
his side, staring into the Hogan's earthen adobe and sandstone wall. The angle of the rays of sun on the floor from the
small opening in the roof told him that it was past seven in
the evening. Grateful for the rest, his level of strength craved
food and replenishment. Yesterday's strain and stiffness had
finally left him.

From habit, he closed his eyes again and lay perfectly
still. In those moments, he gave his other senses time to wake
up. Experience and instincts were responding to something
that had not yet registered in his mind, a presence behind
him, moving across the century-old, hardened, shiny, dirt
floor. In another moment, his ears told him that a snake was
within inches of his face. So much as a flicker of his eyelids
might cause it to strike. It continued. Now brushing his boot,
it rattled ever so slightly. He surmised it was a young rattlesnake looking for food.

The corn pollen in his prayer bag must be the food
that the snake sensed. The bag sat directly across from
him, against the Hogan wall. He smiled internally. Yesterday's bath in the cedar tree was surely part of the spirit's

protection at this moment. As the snake moved around his boot and out of sight, grandfather's arm slowly reached out and tipped the bag towards the wall of the Hogan. Should the snake strike at this moment he was hoping that the thickness of his boot would save him from its poison. No strike. The slithering, again, continued up behind him, around his head and stopped. The rattle paused. The snake sensed the pollen and made its movements toward the opening of the sack. Ever so slowly, it entered.

When Grandfather thought that it had disappeared, he opened his eyes. Like an arching crane, the old man's arm reached the bag and came down on its opening in a flash. Immediately, the sack erupted with a terrible threshing, the rattle shattering the silence of the Hogan. The canvas bag proved impenetrable to the snake's fangs. After a time, the snake retreated and coiled at the bottom of the bag. This allowed Grandfather the time to bring himself up into a sitting position and seal the opening with both hands. He was now safe.

Calmly, the old man walked the prayer sack the half mile to the base of the mesa, where he placed it on the ground next to a large pile of sandstone rocks. He stepped safely back and watched the snake emerge into the rocks and sparse vegetation. Now, with gratitude, he accepted the fact that the spirits of his people had saved him from the ambitions of the skin walker.

As he returned to the Hogan, he gathered particles of nature into the prayer bag—crushed limbs from the cedar brush, leaves of the scrub oak, droppings from rabbits, dried sheep dung, sand and gravel, and ashes from the fires of previous religious ceremonies. All of these he shook together while muttering a petition to his forebears. Without explanations to anyone, he passed throughout the compound of homes, spreading the contents around the doors and into the room of open Hogans, being sure to rub the contents in and around Tanya's and his own entrances. Eventually, he returned to the Hogan and the supper that Tanya had placed by the door.

He sat outside with his back against the logs of the old structure. The silence of North Chapel disturbed him. All of the vehicles had left church. No children played; no sheep and goats brayed because youngsters were trying to lasso them; no vehicles crossed the cattle guard coming back from Saw Tooth with groceries for the extended families.

With the increased darkness, Milton arrived with Robert. The old man knew it was Milton because he drove his truck all the way down to the other side of the Hogan. Neither spoke. The silence conveyed the importance of the coming hours. It also told him what success Milton had experienced in reading the troublesome reservation signs for the people he had visited that day.

Milton placed a bundle of small cedar sticks behind where he would sit in the Hogan. With some of these, in the traditional way, he started a fire using flint in the pit below the opening in the ceiling. He took an elk hide from the truck. He put it in the corner facing the door. As the smoke rose from the fire through the roof's opening into the sky, it formed a cloud, like a wall, between that far corner and the door. With all prepared, Milton sat next to the old man outside for a while, letting the night guide them. Finally, he told him. "Tanya will be ready when she hears the Pinos leave. The spirit of John Sedillo waits by the door. It is time."

Entering the Hogan, the two old brothers led Robert through the Wall of Smoke to the elk hide. Grandfather further concealed the hunter. He took some of the ashes from the fire and made a paste with his spittle. Chanting a song about the spirit and strength of the elk, he rubbed the color of shadows on the hands and face of John Sedillo's spirit. The scent of the elk hide entwined with the rising smoke within the structure of earth-covered logs and beckoned their minds and hearts to all spirits at one with Mother Earth.

For the next hour, Milton and Grandfather sang the Navajo songs, along with the spirits of their forebears, keeping the fire and its Wall of Smoke in place with the small sticks from the bundle of cedar. Robert sat erect, showing a respect for these men from his father's era. Their manner gave evidence of their kind of priesthood. They were unfolding a very simple but important ritual of fire and smoke. Their words spoke of how the earth is renewed by fire, how life depends on its presence for heat, food, and growth. Fire, they acknowledged, can reach across the canyon of life and death because the fire, now in the smoke, rises where it will.

The rattle of the cattle guard told the old men that the Pinos had arrived. When the ritual reached a point of fire consuming evil, Milton went to the truck and escorted the Pinos to the door of the Hogan. As they entered, Grandfather was standing, facing them, the fire and the smoke between them. His arm extended through the smoke, pointing to a place, directly opposite of him, where the three Pinos were to sit.

Woodson, with the wooden leg, found it easier to lie on his side than to sit. The Pinos, who had turned to the Baptist Christian religion when Willow Sr. and Margery were married, wore no traditional clothing for the ceremonial Hogan. The harsh set in their faces and the posture of their stiff bodies portrayed the hostility that they held for these men and this meeting. There was no reverence for the old man or for the ceremony in progress. Their fear had brought them. In their pride, they wished themselves to be elsewhere.

Milton returned to the elk skin and continued to chant slowly and almost inaudibly as Grandfather spoke to the

Pinos. "I tell you that the evil one has visited our reservation. He came and killed my grandson, Lodge. The cause of this evil will be stopped by its own medicine. You believe not what I say. I know. But you must tell me and the spirits of our People what it is that the evil one possesses."

Margery and Willow immediately protested the implication that they knew anything about their daughter's death. At any moment, they feared that they might actually be accused of causing her death. In indignation, they began to leave. "This old man is senile and out of his head," they whispered as they got to their knees.

Grandfather's hand suddenly shot through the smoke and commanded them with a harsh voice. "Silence!" Like a sledgehammer had hit them, they dropped back to the earthen floor.

Grandfather shifted his attention to Woodson and could see that the answer to his question about Katy was in the crippled man's heart. Instead of trying to rise like his parents in protest, Woodson had shrunk more deeply into the floor, trying to make himself smaller. Speaking sternly in the direction of the parents, Grandfather said, "Willow, you leave now with your wife. Woodson stays."

They did as he commanded. Milton's chant changed to a higher pitch and the words now spoken by Grandfather were all in an ancient form of Navajo. Panic grew in Woodson as the tenor of the chant and the spoken words seemed to interact and move toward him like arrows. His head pressed against the earthen floor, his eyes closed tightly, and his body braced as if waiting for a final, violent blow.

Suddenly, the chanting stopped and Woodson, unable to handle the silence, screamed in Navajo, "Her riding blanket, her riding blanket, her riding blanket."

"You shall speak of nothing else until the evil one and his bad blood have left our reservation." Grandfather's voice was a harsh, authoritative whisper, in sharp contrast to Woodson's sobbing cries and gulps for air. His hand again came through the smoke, grabbed Woodson's hair, and pulled his head so that his eyes were just inches from the burning embers. Wailing in pain from the searing smoke and heat, Woodson imagined blindness. The whispered words rang like bells in Woodson's ears. "Go to your silence." Grandfather released his hair.

Woodson fell back from the fire, crawled to the door, and dragged himself out into the darkness. His prosthesis, having come loose from the stub of his leg, trailed off to the side. His parents, hurrying and fearful, quickly got to him and drove off into the night. Unlike their Christian psalms dictate, they entered into the valley of darkness with unimaginable fear. The only words they heard were Woodson's moan, "Her riding blanket, her riding blanket."

The ceremonial Hogan was now silent. Robert's mind still remained his own, but his senses were now absorbed in the sounds, the music, the words, and the energy of the ceremony. Milton had gone for Tanya. He listened as Grandfather prayed with the spirits, repeating what he had learned about Katy's riding blanket. He chanted his belief that the evil one had prepared and intended to kill both his grandson and his wife. Both of the families had been cursed.

Now, more than ever, it was necessary that the spirits of their fathers protect the hunter as he sought out the evil one on Horse Mountain to reverse the curse. He rose slowly and walked back and forth from the fire to the hunter, singing in a whisper of words which, he prayed, would put the fire of the stars into the heart of the hunter. Robert realized, for the first time, that the ceremony, begun here in the Hogan, was going to end with his hunt somewhere on Horse Mountain.

As Milton and Tanya entered the Hogan, Grandfather's hand again pierced the smoke and pointed to the place where she was to sit. It was next to him, affirming her months of learning his way while in the desert with him and the sheep. She sat, now, within the Wall of Smoke, one with the ancient spirits of her people. Her erect position, with bowed head, attested to the pride in her heart and the reverential fear before those of the past whom she believed to be present around her. She listened to Grandfather and Milton as they chanted the strengths of Lodge Tom, strengths that had come to him from the spirits of his forebears.

When her time came, she began her chant without the slightest effort. She thanked Lodge for being the father whom she had never had, for protecting her against the world as she grew up without a mother by her side, for guiding her now during this time of uncertainty. She recognized that it was his strength that had allowed her to take her place as the head of the family in the church meeting earlier in the evening. Although he was gone, the spirit of their family would continue on in his older children, whom she would try to raise. She would bring to them whatever care she could in whatever way possible.

As Tanya grew silent, the two old men each placed additional sticks on the fire. They brought Robert down from the shadows and seated him on the other end of the elk hide, directly in front of the Wall of Smoke. The three, grandfather, Milton, and Tanya, sat in a semi-circle behind him. As Robert looked up, stars were visible through the opening in the roof.

Milton spoke first. "You are now the Hunter. The Hunter has heard the hearts of all concerned tonight. Hunter, you will destroy this evil one. Grandfather found him on Horse Mountain. Feather will take you to his trail tonight. Just follow the reservation boundary. Leave Feather hobbled at Donkey Springs for your return."

Grandfather then spoke his final words. He now told them how the skin walker had tried to kill him with a rattlesnake, pointing to the opening in the earthen roof where it had entered. In the shadows, Robert's eyes sensed the fear and tenseness in both Milton and Tanya. The old man prayed, "Let the spirit of your father guide you to the evil one. Hunter, kill it. Burn it and everything you wear on the side of Horse Mountain. Make this elk hide your only clothing for the ride home. The people must see the fire.

"There, on the mountain, you will find Katy's riding blanket. Hang it on the gate at the southern boundary of the reservation for all who have eyes to see. We shall be here. Hunter, look through your father's eyes, the eyes of John Sedillo, and you will see nothing to fear. The Wall of Smoke, like this one, will protect you."

Still, no one moved. Lodge's sister, Tanya, was to have the last word. "Great spirits, take the Hunter to the hunted. Let the Wall of Smoke be his protection and shield. Make no further harm come to our people."

The Hunter was then left alone before the Wall of Smoke.

CHAPTER 20

North Chapel
Tuesday evening

Now in her rocker, quiet and alone with her thoughts, Tanya lived again the soul-wrenching moments of the day. The valley beyond the open door was starlit darkness and very still. The night offered a backdrop to the vivid ceremonial fire, moments ago, with Grandfather, the Hunter, and Milton. The memory now flowed through her mind and crowded out the ache that fought to rise up again from within. There was now hope and, with that, strength from the spirits of the people. Strange, but she was not frightened by all of it; on the contrary, she was at peace.

How sad, Lodge, that you never experienced the ancient ones of your people. And how different from our exposure to the Christian churches. Tanya, the baptized Christian, could hardly be reconciled with Tanya who lives so intimately with the spirits of her people in a ceremonial Hogan composed simply of earth offerings, such as soil, stones, and wood. And yet, Grandfather does it all of the time.

Each Sunday he sits in church, up front, off to the right, facing the people, reading the Bible. He never leads the Christian ceremonies but certainly is the authority behind the minister whom he had called to serve in North Chapel. She resolved that she would continue to attend Sunday services simply out of respect for her grandfather and in the hope of learning what he found in the Christian rituals.

When she left the ceremony, her grandfather had requested that she tell Francis John II how Feather must be prepared for another nocturnal journey. As she had rounded the house, the man/boy was sitting on the corral fence eating a tortilla. His feet were caught on the lower railing so that he sat relaxed in a position that allowed him to see through the alleyway of the houses down to the ceremonial Hogan. "What does Grandfather need?" he asked, as she approached.

"Will Feather be hard to find tonight?"

"By herself she came in earlier. Not many times she does this. It seems like she can hear the whispers from the Hogan. I don't hear, but I can feel them."

Unbridled, Feather stood silent and quiet as the night, not a hundred yards directly below the corral. As he had done earlier yesterday morning, Francis John took the bridle off the fence and this time with a piece of his tortilla rather than the cornmeal, he raised his arm and walked to Feather.

The stars lit the two silhouettes as horse and boy became one. Together, within a moment, the sound of the hooves moved towards her. She then turned away to her vigil as Francis hoisted Lodge's saddle up from the fence and onto Feather's back, leaving her prepared for the Hunter's mission.

Moments later, Feather's hooves broke the silence. Pounding the earth with the strength of their spirits, horse and Hunter passed the back of Tanya's house on their way up to the mesa. After a time, the click on the rocks from Feather's hooves was barely audible in the distance, and then gradually faded away. Sound carried down the face of the mesa like the surface of a lake. She could imagine the Hunter looking down on her right now and she wondered what it meant for him to be out there in the night, not as Robert but as the spirit of John Sedillo. The man who entered the Hogan was Robert. The man in the saddle on top of the mesa was John Sedillo's spirit.

Does he question it? Does he believe that faith in the spirits of the People can change reality for the good of the People? I pray that the ancient ones will favor him and allow him to share in the greatness of his moment, to understand that Nature does not act against itself. The deaths of Lodge and Katy personified a violent overthrow of life's flow by an enemy of Nature. Perhaps Robert will never put it all together. But, after tonight's hunt he will surely never be the same. The spirits have made him one with his forefathers.

Others of her relatives in the compound must also be listening to the clicks of Feather's footsteps on the rocks above. In the Navajo character, the people never come, never ask questions about the ceremonies or about Milton's truck coming in and going out for the past two days. Is it their fear, or their trust? More than anything, Tanya felt it was the inevitability of life's events that held no room even for their curiosity. For so many generations the People had endured and had confidence that, no matter what, they would continue in spite of what may or may not be.

Was this why her mother did not come to the church this evening, acknowledging that Lodge, who died, is not the Lodge to whom she had given birth? Others had raised him, nurtured him, and paved the way for his life and now his death. More than anything, her mother's years off the reservation had severed her bond with the other women of the reservation whose privilege and right it is to bury their dead.

Even though it was rather bold of her to assume this right that normally rests with the mother of the deceased, Tanya knew in her heart that she, alone, felt what agony Lodge went through at the moment of his death. The circumstances of the death she did not know, nor did she really care to understand. Whatever they were, Lodge was alone when he died.

No bond, no peace, no family, no awareness of the old ones who awaited him. In her empathy with her brother, she felt entitled to the community position that she had rightfully claimed earlier this evening.

For a long moment, she sat motionless, as if listening for something from the absolute silence that surrounded her. But it was an internal disturbance that she heard, something that her grandfather had said in church months ago, maybe years ago, about the weeping women and the tomb of Jesus. *We are not Jews,* he had said. *But like them, we are a people who weep for their dead. These women of the Bible already knew that Jesus was not in the tomb. They went there to show his absence to others. The weeping women were already in touch with the now-living Jesus. This is the power of the People's weeping women, to speak with their dead.*

Lodge, we are closer now than ever before. Should you wish to tell me about the events leading up to your death, I will be here. I will listen to no one else's version but yours, when you are ready. In the meantime, I will follow Grandfather's Way and pray for the success of the Hunter in the hills behind the reservation. With his return, maybe you will feel freer to speak to me.

Now Tanya understood one reason why Grandfather read the Bible, and that was to verify the ways of his People, to hear the Great One speaking directly to his People. Before she fell asleep, she relived Grandfather's encounter with the snake. The hunter must kill the evil one. Otherwise, it would continue to threaten those who weep for their dead.

CHAPTER 21

Saw Tooth
Tuesday night

"I cannot tell you how glad I am to be away from that fucking reservation, especially from that tobacco-slurping, Indian-loving cop. In about two very expressive words, I can tell you what to do with this investigation. Fuck it. Capital Fuck It."

By the time Jefferson had reached "Capital Fuck It," the volume of his voice had risen to its maximum. He threw his head back on the headrest with a violent thump, emotionally geared and ready for any objection from MacDonald.

MacDonald didn't say a word. He continued the drive back to the motel in Saw Tooth, focused as though he were in the fourth turn of the Indianapolis speedway.

When Miguel had gone to take the pictures of the so-called animal print in the anthill, he and Jefferson looked over what was left of a sanitized crime scene in Lodge's house. As soon as Miguel was out of earshot, Jefferson had opened up his frustrations and MacDonald had ordered him, in the strongest of terms, to cool it until they got into the car. Clearly, any further work with Miguel was over for the day.

"Miguel, this end of the team has had it for the day," MacDonald said upon Miguel's return from the old woman's backyard. "We will meet at the Chapter House tomorrow at, say, about 10:30. Maybe you could write up your report. We will do the same and then compare notes in the morning." On leaving Miguel's van after the ride back to the Chapter House for their car, MacDonald added, "We plan to meet with Tilden at the sheriff's office or someplace in Saw Tooth tomorrow before coming up here. Also, the feds are sending someone down from Albuquerque each evening. This film will be picked up tonight and we should have the results by this time tomorrow."

"I hope that it stays quiet tonight. I could use a night's rest," were Miguel's final words.

MacDonald's mind was now back with Jefferson. "I'm sorry about the threat back there, but I couldn't let Miguel know our attitude on the investigation at this time. In part, I agree with you. But, we have to keep our cards close to the chest for a while longer."

"I know, Mac. I'm cooler now, but I still have the same feelings and the same conclusions. Mac, that fucking place is haunted. It is just unreal." The intensity of his feelings broke off each word with surreal mechanics that matched the twisted sounds of his voice.

"If I didn't know better, I'd say that you were experiencing a tad of culture shock. That's for young people, not for us old warriors." He wanted Jeff to understand his empathy without condoning his conduct. The guy just couldn't let it go. It spoke of an ill tide.

"Mac, I'm serious. Just listen, will you? It started with that secretary. We both knew before we got up there that she was Lodge's sister. Now, did she admit it? Hell, no! What the fuck was she doing working in the first place, caught up as she is in the violent death of her brother and sister-in-law? And this one really pisses me off! Did Miguel draw that little fact about Tanya to our attention? No, he did not. Are these people just stupid, out of touch, or what?"

MacDonald was following his argument but he was concerned more with Jefferson's perceptions. To help him vent even more, Mac said, "Well, you have to admit that your observations about Tanya and Miguel go along with Miguel's theory; namely, you don't start off investigating the relatives. You end up with them."

"And let me tell you, I don't buy that bullshit either, not for a fucking minute." Feeling himself getting unnerved even more, Jefferson didn't say another word until they crossed the cattle guard off of the reservation. Then, as though he was now in fresh air and away from some cloud of dread and dust, he went back, more settled, to talk about the day. "Look, Mac, let me go at this from the get go. What did you see at the trading post sitting in Miguel's van while he brought groceries? Did you see any visiting between the adults, any children playing around, any natural exchanges between people? The grandmothers were the ones leaving the trucks. The kids propped up like pieces of plastic in the truck beds. The men slouched down behind the wheels of the vehicles, baseball caps shielding their eyes. Did you see one young, attractive woman? Every woman looked old and very heavy. Their heads were down, beat, forgotten, overweight, sagging breasts, dressed in gym sweats, some even chewing tobacco like Miguel. Compare that scene to the picture of Katy on the wall at the crime scene. A startling contrast, right? A real take out, isn't it? There was sexuality in Lodge's lady." Jefferson knew he was painting a pretty ugly picture of people he had just met. Yet, he felt that this was all taking him someplace; somewhere he knew that the investigation had to go.

"Dead, Mac, that's it. Dead." Jefferson was pointing at the land around him. "See those junipers? Dried up. Dead. Section after section of dead or dying trees. A land deserted by a living, giving, sustaining substance. Dried up. I'm telling you, Mac, the dead land is a symbol of the people back there. They are history. Something is over for Twin Rivers, with nothing in the future. Katy, from her picture at least, was alive, going, and had a tomorrow. Maybe that's what has me so angry. Twin Rivers killed any and all challenges to its deadness."

They remained silent until the car stopped at the Mountain High Motel. "I'm buying," Mac offered. "Let's walk back to the Cow Hide Bar for a drink. Maybe you can wash the taste of Twin Rivers out of your mouth."

"You know, taste is a great analogy. I'm convinced that Miguel keeps that shit in his mouth so that he cannot taste or smell Twin Rivers." It gave Jefferson a great deal of pleasure to see Miguel, even in his imagination, in a defensive mode about that damn place.

In its day, the Cow Hide had seen five killings. The last one had been ten years ago. As though ready for the next one, the floor was covered by fresh saw dust and peanut shells. The shells came from bowls of salted peanuts that sat on the bar. They made a crunching sound as MacDonald and Jefferson approached it to order a drink. The bar stretched from the door clear across the length of the room. A sign on it read, "Longest Bar West of the Mississippi. Shipped from Kansas City, Missouri, 1888."

Another reason for the sawdust was the mess around the spittoons just inside the foot railing at the base of the bar. *God*, Jefferson thought. *Alonzo must love this place with all of that shit on the floor.* Nodding his head toward the spittoons, Jefferson leaned over and whispered to MacDonald, "I'll bet the kids around here are weaned on Copenhagen."

The back of the bar had the usual naked lady relaxing on her couch, surrounded with bottles, glasses, and a mirror that no longer reflected images from the bar. It offered a cracked and splintered pattern from previous encounters with bullets, thrown objects, and probably the head of a human being or two. This décor was bordered on three sides by shelves of dusty glasses painted with what appeared to be a century of flyspecks.

The two men ordered scotch on the rocks. The barmaid reached down and brought up a dusty bottle of Johnny Walker's Red Label and slammed it down in front of Jefferson with a short gaggle. "I don't get much call for this juice in here nowadays. Here, let me wipe it clean for you." She reached down and grabbed her dress, pulled it up to the level of the bar and turned the bottle in its dirty folds. "You just take the bottle with you, now, and I will charge you on what you used on the way out." With that, she turned, pulled two glasses from behind her, and sat them next to the bottle. "You strangers will learn our ways soon enough." Apparently, ice had not yet found its way to Saw Tooth's Cow Hide. Whiskey was straight up and straight down. At least the glasses did not appear to be of the fly-shit class.

Maybe it was his sensitivity to the strangeness of the past few days, but the face of that woman was really unlike any that he had encountered for a long time. MacDonald looked at the deep wrinkles swarming from every aperture in her face. The huskiness of her voice testified to her years of smoking. But it was the perkiness in the voice that was so out of character when compared to the face, the throat, and her presence in this "cultured" hole of a bar.

The perkiness was like that of his teenage daughter on the night of her first date. But God, his daughter in the Cow Hide! The contrast gave him a passing moment of queasiness, one that rises when certainty recognizes the irreconcilable. Closing his eyes, he gently shook his head in disbelief. Jefferson interrupted his reverie by tapping his shoulder and pointing to the glasses. "Come on, there might be a table in the back."

"Pull up a chair, gentlemen. Relax in the ways of the cowboys and breathe in the air of old-time Saw Tooth. My name is Pat Wade, and you are the two federals investigating Lodge's killings. What are your names?"

Two chairs came sliding out from the table with the same feet that had hooked them a moment earlier and kept Fred and Jake Farley from sitting down. Wade had seen the two federal officers walk in and wanted to introduce himself. Wade's table had seen him every evening for the past eight years. Semi-retired after nearly forty years in federal government jobs, he was now working at the Twin Rivers Navajo School Board's vocational-education program.

MacDonald's first thought was, *A little local color never hurt anyone.* "Thank you, Mr. Wade. You have the advantage on us," Jefferson said, while taking in yet another surprise and letting the professional cop take over.

"Don't mean to. I just saw you today with Miguel at Twin Rivers and had heard that the feds were checked in at the Mountain High. Glad that I got a chance to talk to you." Without interrupting his flow of conversation, Pat Wade reached over and took the glasses and the bottle of scotch that Jefferson had put on the table. He held them off to the side and splashed whiskey inside and out, shaking them as if drying them some before placing everything back on the table. "I always throw the first one on the floor. You cannot believe how dirty that lady's hands can really get." With that, he poured the glasses, his own included, half full.

"You're right about the Twin Rivers investigation. Did you know Lodge or his wife, Katy?" MacDonald followed, grateful that the dilemma of the woman's dirty dress was so easily handled.

"Well enough, after working with Lodge for eight years, to know that he would never kill himself. He might kill Katy, but never himself. More than likely, if Lodge killed anyone, it would be that silly-assed brother-in-law of his. Scary, sorry sonofabitch, is what he is." The words "son of a bitch" flowed through his nasal passages. "In my mind, that bastard has already killed once before and is probably somewhere behind Lodge and Katy's deaths."

The first real information of the day. And where does it come from? From a western character in the pits of a Saw Tooth bar, thought Jefferson. As the whiskey found its way down, he warmed to this man's hospitality and candor. He followed up, "You are talking about Woodson, Katy's brother, aren't you?"

The question hung out there like the smell of tobacco juice as Pat got up and jerked his way over to the bar. It was hard to tell just where the stiffness actually was in Pat's five-foot ten-inch frame because, as one side of him went up, the other side kind of convulsed in a mild spasm. He reached over the bar and grabbed a bowl of peanuts and ambled back. He kind of threw himself back into his chair, not spilling a single nut from the bowl. "Goddam arthritis is hell in my right heel," he said.

"Look," he continued, "did anybody tell you that Lodge had just purchased a new $35,000 Ford pickup, about four weeks ago? Now that is a dream come true for any Indian man. Throw away a wife but never a new truck. In that truck, Lodge was the cock of the walk out there." With that, he knocked down about a third of his whiskey. A relaxed smile appeared just under his glasses, which had slipped down on his nose. He pushed the glasses and the rim of his hat up in the same motion that also wiped his wrist across his lips with a guttural sigh of pleasure. Such a gesture was built on years of practice.

"Yes, we saw the pickup, right by the back door. Crime people said that no keys have shown up as yet. Miguel explained it to us," Jefferson said, knowing that he was lying about Miguel but kept it in a way that was meant to encourage his new friend to continue. Wade did not need encouragement.

"My question for you *federales* is, where in hell did he get the down payment? Had to be what, four or five thousand dollars? He'd never saved that kind of money on his salary. The two extended families on each side together could never save that much money. All of them are on welfare and jewelry-making. I bet you a bottle of scotch that the source of that money is tied to their murders."

By this time, MacDonald had finished his second scotch and felt a bit challenged that this beat-up old cowboy was directing an investigation from a knife-scarred table in the seediest bar in New Mexico, if not the entire Southwest. "Let's not talk of murders for a moment, but rather of killings. It keeps our options open. For example, maybe there was an accident involved, or are you pretty sure of the murder thing?" Did Wade have some kind of witness in mind?

A smile appeared in Wade's features, one wrinkle at a time, first in the lines of his eyes, then in the corner of his mouth. "Let me tell you what a killing is. See that hole and crack at the bottom left side of the mirror there, behind the bar?" As they looked over, the three men saw the woman from behind the bar come through an inside door on their far right.

"Somebody get Bubba a free drink," she shouted. The entire place went up in a round of cheers, shrieks, and laughter. Chairs banged on the floor and fists beat the bar in a hearty roar of demands.

The two feds gaped in wonder, watching Wade set down his glass with whisky sloshing all over. Tears formed in his eyes and he gasped for another emphysema breath, all from laughing so hard. "I'll give it to you straight, men," he said. "The lady has just given Bubba his monthly service in the lady's room back there. Do you see why I washed your glasses?" This turned Wade's face red again with a suppressed cry for oxygen. "You oughta see your faces right about now." Wade finally choked it out. The two feds broke up, almost tipping themselves back out of their chairs. They laughed at themselves, at Wade, and at the stupid fucking situation they were in; and, it felt good, very good, indeed.

"Where was I now? Oh, yes. I was going to tell you about a killing and the difference between that and a murder." Wade had recovered enough to continue his story. "When I was growing up around here, I came into this bar whenever I come to town with my Pa. I was only nine or ten. One afternoon I watched Johnny McGraw put a slug into and through Cap Smith's neck. Out it came from Cap's neck and right into that glass mirror, like I said, that you see over there to your left. Now, that was a killing because Smith had been taunting McGraw and looking at him in the mirror while McGraw sat over there playing cards, with his back to Smith." Wade pointed to the second table toward the back of the room. "Everybody at that table thought it would be better if they took a pee break. Nobody at the bar, though, moved; and that, right there, should have told Cap something; but he didn't pick up on it. Finally, when everybody was clear of the table Johnny said in a loud, clear voice, 'Fuck you, Cap.'

"Smith's hand dropped to his holster and started up with his revolver. In the same motion, his head of red hair had turned toward Johnny's table and his shoulders were ready to whip around square with his gun firing on an extended arm. But his gun didn't clear the holster. A hand was locked on his wrist, right at belt high. McGraw's gun fired at the same moment his chair hit the floor. Johnny and the guy who had held Cap's wrist then walked out the door. 'Tell the sheriff we'll be in town in another month, if he wants us for this killing.'" Wade paused.

"See, that was a killing," he explained. "Planned, pimped, and carried out. Now, Lodge and Katy don't even know anybody that could do that. Whatever went on there in Lodge's house was never intended. So you see it was no killing. It just happened. I think that you *federales* would call it a crime of passion."

This Wade was just too much. Yet Jefferson did not want to offend his host. "Pat, I'll keep your distinction in mind." With this lesson in the difference between killings and murder, Jefferson wanted to get back to Lodge's truck and the financial arrangements for its purchase. "Pat, where do you think the money for the truck came from?" he asked.

"Twin Rivers has only one legitimate source of money in that quantity and that is the Twin Rivers Navajo School Board, Inc.," Wade answered, knowing full well that he had stressed the word legitimate. Jefferson picked up on it. "Legitimate?" he asked.

"The big illegitimate source of money around here in Saw Tooth and in Cuba is drugs. I would not be surprised if Lodge's wife got caught up somehow. She was the only real looker on the reservation, attractive to both Indian and non-Indian. The white people, for sure, at Twin Rivers control both the legitimate and any illegitimate sources of money on the reservation. With that, I have probably said far too much."

"Who are they?" Both had said it at the same time.

"Go to the business office and the school's classrooms. The users are all there." Wade threw down his final shot of whisky and stood up to go. "Come by the trailer tomorrow and we can talk some more. I know that school is out but my students and I have to take care of the ranch and the cattle. I'd get some food on top of that scotch in short order if I were you." As he hobbled out the door, he threw a twenty-dollar bill on the bar and pointed to the bottle of scotch on the table.

Jefferson kicked MacDonald's chair and said, "Fable. That's the word. I think that Wade just "fabilized" us with his bull shit. Felt good, too."

CHAPTER 22

North Chapel
Tuesday Night

The moment that he stepped through the Wall of Smoke and out of the Hogan into the starlit night, Robert began the personal journey toward understanding this new chapter in his life. Except for the elk hide he had strapped behind him, riding out like this into the night for a hunt, be it elk, deer, or bear, was familiar ground. He had camouflaged himself with clothing and grease to resemble the shades of the night, adding to Grandfather's earthen paste. His bow was strapped to the saddle horn for a quick release.

There was ample food for a week in his backpack, and extra water would never be more than a half-day's ride in any direction. He was now in his element. At home with the night, he relaxed for the first time since Milton's visit. The only thing missing on the trail tonight was Jaime, who normally would be just ahead of him. Reaching the top of the mesa, he was now ready to piece together the past twelve hours so that he could get a mindset for the next two or three days.

To start with, Milton had surely tapped him for a "biggie," all because of his father's former position among the elders in the Twin Rivers community. After Milton had left, Jaime had come off the roof right away when Robert had not gone back to the shingling job. Robert had told him about Milton's use of the phrase "spirit of John Sedillo." That is when Jaime had asked Gloria to make coffee and meet him and Robert down at the corrals.

Jaime and Robert were four years apart, of different mothers, in the large family of John Sedillo. Jaime, the thinker, was smaller and slimmer. Robert, the doer, stood taller, stronger, and heavier. Jaime was always the teacher, Robert the student. They accepted their roles, and it had resulted in an indestructible confidence between them.

When Gloria came with the coffee, Jaime began, "What I say, I say only once. It is not for questions to follow. Fabriano and Milton Tom are brothers and among the elders of the Twin Rivers People. You know this. It becomes apparent that these two men have chosen to speak to you about the trouble surrounding Lodge and Katy's deaths. Already waves of fear sweep across the reservation families. As I see it, their speaking now is a confirmation that the ancient spirits of good and evil are loose in the community. Denial of their presence would be a risk to all of us.

"My mother says that many years ago, our father John Sedillo, provided meat to reservation families when they needed it. Always when asked he would leave for three days to hunt. It became a tradition that his return would be signaled in the middle of the second night with a fire on the west end of Horse Mountain. Some believe that he burnt the branded hides of the stolen animals on the mountainside. He would always say that his horse had no room to pack them out.

"Sometimes, on special occasions, Milton would come for John Sedillo, notably to hunt for meat. When this happened, always Fabriano was included. Always it was night, and always the troubled spirits were moving in the midst of the people.

"Today, no one comes to us for meat. Yet, each year we hunt and always we return with meat when many others from Twin Rivers do not. How often we have commented that our father is with us on each and every hunt. And now, for the first time in many years, Milton again seeks a hunter for a special purpose, in the night, with Fabriano, in the midst of the many troubled spirits on the reservation."

Bringing his story to a conclusion, Jaime put his outstretched arms on Robert's shoulders and said, "Robert, I cannot tell you what they hunt. I know that you will be successful. I will look for our father's fire."

Without another word, Jaime went home. Robert and Gloria returned to the house and prepared for Milton's return.

It was well after midnight. Robert reflected on these and other events, climbing into the high country west of the reservation. Feather needed no direction or prodding as she followed the fence line next to the LaDue ranch.

Robert had decided that he would stay on the upper slopes during the day. From that vantage point, he could watch Horse Mountain and the valley below for any signs of movement. Then, at night, he would move down into the valley. In two days' time he could cover the entire mountain.

The weight of the final words of the two old men still hung in his mind. *The evil one. Find it, Hunter, and kill it.* And then, there was the snake. Are we talking human here, or what? Could the Hunter become the hunted? Robert was confident that after the first night he could tell if there was another human being in the mountains. If he detected one, he would simply get the hell out of there. No way would he stalk and pull down an arrow on a person for anybody. Even if he were Lodge's killer, Robert would not be an Indian vigilante committee of one. So the conclusion was easy.

By tomorrow night he would either be gone or set into the hunt for some animal that somehow, at least in the minds of the two old men, was connected to Lodge's death. A lot of Indian people believed that people and animals exchanged powers and skin and stuff. He personally couldn't buy into this faith. Yet, he could do the ceremonial hunt for his people as well as any believer, probably better than most because he wouldn't be distracted. So, if there was an animal out there that symbolized all this evil, left a sign on the earth, then that wasn't faith or belief anymore. A footprint is a real sign in the real earth. That is the hunt. That is the search. That is what I am all about.

Robert took his time dismounting. He was satisfied that he had his head in the right place. Throwing the backpack to the ground, he pulled out a piece of deer jerky and chewed slowly, savoring every bit of the salt, the chili, and wild flavor. The stars told him that there was about two hours until daylight. As though to acknowledge the thought, Feather pawed the ground, showing her eagerness to move on. Robert patted her forehead, picked up the reins and threw himself back up in the saddle. "If I remember right, Feather, you are to show me something along the way. How about getting on with it?"

If he had his bearings right, he calculated that Donkey Springs was about a half mile due south from the ridge he was on. Feather did not stop but chose to head down the fence line going east. "Whatever you say, old gal. I am in your hands," he said, leaning forward and slapping her neck and withers. After another quarter of a mile, Feather stopped short of the third drainage ditch coming north out of the mountains, just inside the tree line. With one body, both horse and rider turned to basic instincts. Silence became the communicator.

While Feather could smell in the silence, Robert could sense from her demeanor what she was experiencing. Her head kept swinging from north to south. The greater danger was to the right. Finally, she brought her hindquarters around so that she stared directly up the slope of the mountain. "Good girl. Steady now," he whispered down her neck. Easily, he backed her further into the trees until he was able to turn her back up the fence line. Her nervousness gradually subsided. When they were far enough back up on the ridge, he turned her toward Donkey Springs.

A smile creased Robert's face as he turned Feather loose, tethered with a long rope. He was ready. He had the starting point, the real thing. Something was down there. It had to have left a trail. Whatever else Grandfather wanted during the ceremony in the Hogan, it would have to take care of itself.

CHAPTER 23

Saw Tooth
Wednesday morning

Breakfast for the two federal officers was at Betty Tilden's café, owned by the deputy sheriff's wife. Jefferson had the three-egg omelet filled with fried potatoes, onions, cheese, and a dash of red bell peppers and smothered in green chili. Added to that was coffee and toast with homemade blueberry jam. With such good food, it was understandable why, at 8 a.m., there wasn't an open table or an empty chair in the place.

MacDonald and Jefferson sat across from John Tilden, the same person who had answered Miguel's call for help early Monday morning. They were together as a result of one of Jefferson's phone calls last night. The other calls were to the BIA office in Albuquerque to be sure that its man was coming, and to his wife.

With the departure of Pat Wade from the Cow Hide, the evening had quickly become a roomful of drunken cowboys with "feudin', fightin', and fuckin'" as the only subjects of consequence. They had placed the empty bottle of scotch back on the bar with another $20 bill protruding from its neck. The lady had disappeared again, probably with another customer. MacDonald had then gone across the street to pick up a pizza from the front porch of Saw Tooth's version of the Pizza Hut, a home serving up pizza from its kitchen oven to a crowd of customers that stretched all the way through the screened-in front porch and down to the curb.

After the small talk of getting acquainted with Tilden, Jefferson brought the conversation to the point. "This is Wednesday. What happened at Twin Rivers? I mean, you've had all of two days to solve that crime on the reservation." The sarcasm was not lost on Tilden.

The deputy spoke with a "twangy" drawl, having come into New Mexico from Texas about five years ago with his wife and two children. "Being stationed up here in Saw Tooth, you cannot believe the number of Twin Rivers Indians I throw into jail every week. For the most part, it is the same ones, but now and then, a new face will surprise me. For example, I took Lodge Tom off the road about three weeks ago. He and his new truck were all over it, just below Twelve Mile Hill."

"Alcohol appears to be the number one neighbor for a good many people around these parts, white as well as Indians. What about hard drugs?" Jefferson knew that alcohol was interwoven with the Indian reservations. What he wanted at this time amounted to a general picture of the drug scene in these parts, including the reservation. It is something a good law officer picks up when working in an area for any length of time. Tilden looked like his best bet.

Certainly, after yesterday's experience on the reservation, he could never trust Miguel's contribution on the subject. Nor were the local citizens in the café this morning likely to be of much help. The ordinary person, the construction workers at BIA, the Forest Service workers, the Twin Rivers families, the retired couples, or the tourists; none of them would give drug use a thought.

"Drug use on the Twin Rivers? Cocaine? Heroine? They are too expensive for the Indians. The white people out there, now, that is another story. They get big salaries and can afford the price. You know about Messenger?" Tilden had to find a starting point with these guys. "His vehicular homicide conviction? Possession and use of all kinds of drugs? Their executive director, a guy by the name of Sussman, convinced the Indian Board to keep Messenger on as the financial manager. Really bad news for the Indians, as well for Messenger who needed rehab treatment more than his job!"

MacDonald nodded, "That was in the file on Twin Rivers. Sketchy. Let's have your general perspective, especially in light of these recent deaths."

Bending his head toward the middle of the table, Tilden spoke in a soft voice. "My theory, gentlemen, and let me emphasize that it is mine, starts out with the fact of entangled law enforcement up there on the reservation. Since the federal government is the principle cause of that stupidity, I going to give it to you straight, no color coating.

"In my opinion," he continued, "Saw Tooth, here, is a major crossroads for hard drugs from Southern California and Arizona." He paused and looked at each man. "Several white, Twin River employees who live up there are part of the traffic routes. The drugs go in a back road and out another back road. I must congratulate these people for their choice of that reservation. They know a legal and jurisdictional sink hole when they find it."

Not a word came from his listeners. They gave their man all the time and space he needed to regroup from what apparently sat deeply in his craw. "I mean, I had no business out there on Monday with Miguel. Really. Did I? The feds have given the entire law-enforcement jurisdiction to the Window Rock tribal police. Correct? No county or state jurisdiction. Miguel represents the only "local" jurisdiction, which by the way, has a jail-and-court system that is only 500 fucking miles away, excuse the French.

"And who were the absolute last to show up at the crime scene on Monday? Right, Miguel's boys from the tribal police. And here's the kicker. Who has jurisdiction over the white folks' activity up there? You, the tribe, the state, me? Practically speaking, 'absolutely, no one' is the correct answer." Tilden sat back, taking his coffee but holding up his hand in a gesture of more to come.

"Now, it is true that the Indians can do whatever they damn well please to these white people on their reservation, and the whites have no recourse. For example, as business-people, their Indian contracts, whether in employment, con-sultancy, or business, are not worth a shit. More French.

"On the other hand, the white people, who hide behind the great gift of the federal government to all Indians known as the tribal sovereignty, can steal everyone right out of their jockeys. And they do. Dealers cannot repossess trucks, mobile homes, or whatever. It is a nightmare's nightmare, and with these new on-reservation casinos opening, it only adds to the chaos. That, gentlemen, is Twin Rivers, according to Tilden." He pushed back his chair, picked up his coffee, and let the feds digest what they had asked for. Tilden was rather proud of himself because he had never quite put it like this. But then, he had never talked to a fed about a murder at Twin Rivers, either.

"Are you telling us that Lodge or Katy or both were part of your drug trafficking and sovereignty theories?" Jeffer-son, trying to get the conversation back to Lodge and Katy, formed the question very deliberately. If the feds accepted Tilden's angle, then so many possibilities for the "who" in this crime would be opened. DEA and INA in this area? Unlikely! Tilden could have it right. About as safe a location as you could find for druggies.

"No, I don't really think that Lodge and Katy had anything to do with drugs. They were not users. I'd have known that.

Besides, their death scene up there is mighty different from any of our other local, drug-related murders. In some ways, and this is just my opinion, their killings were almost staged, for publication. It was like saying, 'Don't fuck with me.'"

Tilden was winding down now but he knew that his listeners still had not yet gotten the right picture on the drugs. "The local users and dealers in Cuba and Saw Tooth know that some reservation employees are going through the Twin Rivers with drugs. However, these little mules do not supply the local needs. No, no. The local stuff comes via El Paso, Texas. 'What is the basis for this distinction?' you might ask. In the past year, alone, three local murders were directly connected to the El Paso group. In fact, two of the local dealers, one of them the husband of a Twin River employee, left Saw Tooth after the last murder that took place down in Cuba. He felt that his sorry ass was next."

Jefferson and MacDonald looked at each other with a glance that said, Is he or isn't he? Let's find out. "Where does Miguel fit into this picture of the reservation area being used as a depot for drugs?"

"Miguel and his family live out there. His real backup, as I said, is 500 miles away. I think that both the tribal police and the white burros just ignore him. Now, I have nothing against you two guys personally; but the feds, as I said before," here Tilden paused for dramatic effect, "have made Twin Rivers the pissing rock of the Southwest. Now, it's the druggies' turn, and they are continuing the national tradition in a royal manner."

As if on cue, they rose with him, shook hands, and Tilden turned to leave without another word. Jefferson walked to the door with him. "One more question. Does Miguel know of your idea?" he asked.

"I don't think so. He sees it a little differently," Tilden told him.

Jefferson came back to his chair. "I need another cup of his wife's coffee. Do you buy Tilden's ideas?"

Mrs. Tilden responded to his raised hand; and, after she poured, the little woman surprised them with a quiet little giggle and slid into the empty chair. "John did not hold back any of his cards, did he? I can always tell. When he leans into the middle of the table, it is the Twin Rivers thing eating at him. He wouldn't want that family over there to be hurt by overhearing him. Have you asked yourself why he feels so strongly?"

Dumbfounded might be the word to express the looks on the faces of two master detectives. The Tildens could certainly read each other. Answering her own question, Amy Tilden continued, "OK. It is quite easy. You see, five years ago I was hired by the school board up there, on a three-year contract, as their school principal. They fired me after two years. Reason? I demanded that Sussman use tens of thousands of dollars in their private interest account for the kids' education, not for the administration's personal slush fund. Out I went, and what really hurts is that tribal sovereignty protected Sussman's ass just like he was an Indian…or did John already tell you that the New Mexico District Court refused to hear our case against Sussman and the School Board?"

Remarkable. Jefferson heard his own feelings about Twin Rivers behind the stories of these two people. Not that he agreed with the federal responsibility thing. But, hell, that was somebody else's worry.

"Mrs. Tilden, you and John are pretty rough on our kind. Can you—"

"Listen, I got to get back to work," she said, cutting him off. "Come back tonight. I'll show you Indian magic…how all Indian funds, education or whatever program, all turn into welfare dollars."

"Wait, wait. How about two roast beef sandwiches and a cup of your insight for lunch?"

She nodded OK. "Take a look at the sign by the cash register on the way out." As requested, the detectives did so. It read: "Twin Rivers is Red...not Red, White, and Blue." Free copies of the District Court's decision on "Tilden vs. Twin Rivers School Board" lay beside it.

CHAPTER 24

Saw Tooth Mountains
Wednesday morning

Feather was secure, with plenty of grass and water. Hobbling could make a problem for her with a bear or a large cat that might take advantage of her inability to run or strike back with her front feet. On the other hand, if something happens to the rope, she might wander away, a chance he would have to take. Kneeling in the shadows of a pine tree, after placing the saddle and elk skin in its lowest crotch, he checked the contents of his backpack: jerky, spotting scope, fire makings, heavy nylon line, plastic rain gear, and moccasins.

On his belt hung a hatchet, a knife, and a canteen. Standing now, he attached his compound bow with its internal quiver of arrows to a harness dangling from his left shoulder. In a silvery flash, the sharp edges of the arrows' broad heads caught the light of the late-appearing moon, assuring Robert that they could deliver death to any life through internal bleeding caused by severed veins or arteries.

The nature of a bow hunt would normally give him plenty of time to judge what he would do after spotting his game. The first step, then, in this hunt, was putting himself in a position overlooking the entrance to the north drainage where Feather had stopped. That observation point would be crucial. The plan was simple after that. Spot and stalk the animal's run. Make sure there were no surprises. Get to its pathway and then let the target come to you. At this point, Robert could find no reason to change this time-proven approach. It had led to the kill of many fine animals. Shaking his head from the need to sleep, he told himself that he would rest later, in the warmth of tomorrow's sun.

Robert looked up the side of the mountain. Before sunrise, he needed to be on its top and settled in. Slowly and noiselessly, he began the steep climb with one careful step after another, not going straight up but angling to his right, which made it a more gradual ascent. Every forty or fifty paces he stopped, leaning back on a tree or squatting behind a bush, and looked in every direction for any sign of movement. He was still as the trees, waiting and listening. The finger of scrub oak where Feather grazed was still visible in the moonlight over his left shoulder. Nothing stirred.

After an hour and eight or so ascents, Robert saw what he was looking for, a saddle that offered access to the top of the ridge. It was to his left and above him, about one hundred yards from where he now stood. One or two more silent pushes and he would be over the top.

The saddle offered him a grassy slope. Before moving up and over, he sat down and listened to the nocturnal sounds of life as they drifted over the edge of the ridge. Once up on top, his hunt would begin. Robert reflected that one of the usual elements of a hunt, its anticipation, was not pumping in his bloodstream. A certain amount of the unexpected had been replaced with the certainty of something strange. It all stemmed from the moment Milton had called him to be the spirit of John Sedillo, and through the recent religious ceremony with the old men a few hours ago.

Connecting his presence on the mountain with the ceremonial event dulled the brightness of the unforeseen and replaced it with an awareness of a personal danger associated somehow with the deaths of Lodge and Katy. Robert berated himself because he knew that if he did not control this flow of emotion, he would not win the contest with the hunted. So he must acknowledge the conflict and move beyond it quickly.

Staying bent low, he broke the horizon of the ridge in such a gradual manner that nothing more than a moving moonlight shadow pinpointed his location. He continued across the ridge until he sensed a descent from the highest point to his left. The ridge was very narrow, and if he could inspect the ground under his feet, he was certain that he would find a lot of deer droppings. Soon, light would break over the ridge of Horse Mountain, which loomed over him to the east. By then, he had to be completely hidden and stay that way until the sun filled the valley below. Otherwise, his movements would reflect the light to any life beneath him.

He knew that the farther south he walked, the better his view of the drainage to the north should be. If he were lucky, he could find a spot that looked both ways, north and south, as well as down into the canyon. Staying close to the east side of the ridge, he finally found what he was looking for, a small, out-jutting of the rocks to his left and away from the line of the ridge. Now, he must wait until the light was overhead. Carefully, he released the bow and laid it on the ground.

Dropping to his knees, he removed the backpack and then sat with his back against a pine tree. With the satisfaction of being in the right position above his prey and well hidden, he reached over and pulled another piece of jerky from the backpack. The red chili on it warmed his throat and moved on up into his sinuses. The combination of chili and wild deer gave him tastes of the comfort of his home, which, on a clear day, if he had a strong telescope, he could probably see from this vantage point. With these thoughts, his head gradually slumped forward and he slept until the heat of the sun on the back of his neck brought him back to his surroundings.

There was no jerking of his head but a gradual straightening as he became conscious of his position. He took in every sound and sight available to his senses. The sounds told him of a squirrel up in the branches to his right, eating something and dropping pieces of it into the undergrowth. A chipmunk was making its way along a log, a log that he remembered crawling across last night.

The gobbling of a turkey behind him was in the valley where he left Feather. It must be at least a quarter of a mile away. He could sense nothing near him that, should it be spooked by his movements, would give away his position. Lowering himself to his stomach, he pulled himself over the grass and pine needles to the edge of the ridge.

As he inched toward a break in the underbrush, his eyes climbed down the crevices and slopes on the mountainside opposite him, looking for any kind of movement that would signify life. One at a time, he removed the rocks ahead of him and placed them to his left. The last thing he needed was a rock falling down into the canyon. The opening broke out to the south, where he saw cattle grazing with their calves, running and kicking, never far from their mothers. A pickup ground its way into the rolling mountains down on the West Gate ranch, about a mile further south, beyond the canyon that tumbled down from the Royal Bluffs area. So far, so good.

He pushed his hands ahead of him as he turned the top half of his body around a large bolder, again picking up the small rocks and putting them off to his left. Slowly, he inched his head out into another opening, this time with a vista of the drainage going to the north. Just what he had hoped for? The valley directly below him was still in the shadow of

Horse Mountain and would be for another hour. That was all right.

Before he could reach out and look down to the floor, he would have to find something to cover the silhouette of his head and his small sighting scope. Then, he would be ready to map out the comings and goings of nature below him. His challenge was to become part of that scene before attempting to remove an animal from its surrounding, taking it quietly with the silence of a deadly arrow.

He moved quickly and soundlessly back and beyond his "camp" to a cedar brush where he effortlessly slashed off several small green branches with his bowie knife. Returning to his backpack, he cut a piece of line and gathered the branches together. He then put them down the back of his coat so that they stuck out over and behind his head. After a long drink of water, he stood up behind the tree and relieved himself. He was now ready for a long look-see down in the valley and up into the north wash.

He moved back to the spot where he looked north. Methodically, he scraped the ground level so that the tripod of the scope could find a level base. As he positioned himself behind it, he thought once again of the hunting ceremony. A certain uneasiness began to creep back. They had prayed with the spirits of their forefathers who had entered (they believed) the Hogan, defined the kill that he should make, and even discovered that part of the cause of Katy's death lay in a horse blanket that dumb Woodson had somehow given away. They had even prayed over his eyes that he would see and find the evil one. He thought, *That part about being able to kill the evil one if I am guided by my father's spirit. What the hell does that mean? You see what you see. Give me another hour and I will be able to tell them what I see within a mile of this ridge.* With that, the uneasiness subsided and he was back to the business of finding whatever was down there.

His usual pattern of surveying an area was from top to bottom, from the ridge to valley. But as he crawled up to the scope, the sights flipped on their loose-fitting axis and he was now looking at the floor of the valley. That was all right. He would reverse the process and scan the side of the mountain from the bottom up. He tightened the knob of the sights to keep it steady.

His first view was of the windmill, water holding tank, and catch basin used for drinking just above the main drainage in the canyon. As he brought the magnification into focus, he was startled to see three dead cows and their calves, all within a circle of one hundred and fifty yards from the water tank. What had happened? There was no sign of a struggle, such as an attack of some kind of wild animal—bear or bobcat. Maybe they were shot. But no, if that were the case, he should see a large dark spot on the ground around the animals, and there was none.

The scene, save for the dead animals, was undisturbed. This early, there was no dust moving. Lengths of rusted iron pipe from previous repairs on the well lay along the corral's fence line. Pieces of black plastic pipe were exposed leading from the water tank in a straight line to the south. It carried the water to another drinking area with its gravity flow. He could not see that drinking area.

Although he could not hear the clank of the windmill, he could imagine it by seeing its periodic pumping action when the gentle breeze rotated the twelve-foot fan. It did not move long enough to bring any water to the surface. There were no tire tracks on the rutted road coming into the area. So, that meant that Mr. Wade and the students from the vocational-education program did not know that their herd had been depleted.

Nature had been whacked. Feather had sensed it. But dead animals would not have brought the horse's startled reaction. Then it dawned. There were no scavengers. Where were the vultures, the coyote, the ripped-open stomachs of the animals? Bloating was present, so the odor had to be horrendous. He rolled away from the sight of the scope and lay looking up through the branches, the blue sky sparkling through the floating pine needles. Nature passed in peace above; nature stalled in carnage below. What was the reason?

The scene below assured him that no human being friendly to the Twin Rivers people was recently in the area. The whole reservation would have known about the dead animals within an hour after they were sighted. Poison. And then, he rolled back to the scope. It was not the season for the poison weeds. They needed the rains that were a couple of months away. And besides, animals died in a struggle when they were poisoned with the likes of locoweed. Maybe the water? He put the scope to full power on the water in the tank. Nothing. He inched the increased power over to the overflow pit that runs from the tank. And look there, two dead birds floating on the surface of the water. Something or someone had apparently poisoned the overflow pit. "Find the evil and destroy it." Grandfather's words. In the old man's mind, the death scene below him and the reason for the death scene in Lodge's house about four miles north were connected. He would leave that connection to others. But from his days of hunting, Robert always respected the beauty of the deer and elk as nature's gift that he had killed and taken from the forest. Something—or someone—evil had killed Lodge and Katy, as well as the animals around that tank. Now, he was supposed to find the evil that caused these deaths. It would depend on a lot of things.

CHAPTER 25

Chapter House
Wednesday morning

Miguel was refreshed after his first full night's sleep since the killings. His notes, hand-written last night, lay on the table, spread out like chess pieces. Each represented a motive, a person, a suspect, or a place. Separating the pieces of the report enabled him to bring the people and motives into Lodge's house. He would ask himself, Do they belong? Is there a real connection? Off to the side lay those who, in his judgment and for various reasons, could not be part of that death scene. *A process of elimination? Maybe*, he answered himself.

Tanya sat across the table from him in the delegates' office of the Chapter House, waiting for the two detectives. "Where am I, Miguel?" she asked, pointing to the table. Not knowing exactly what he was doing, she could tell, nevertheless, that his thoughts included her and the interview that he had told her would take place this morning.

"You will never be on the table. That is, as a suspect. In a few hours, though, what you say will be up here and in the feds' reports, as well. Just speak from the heart so that Lodge becomes a real person for these sons of Washington."

The Chapter door, with its customary crash of metal on metal due to the absence of the hydraulic closer, announced the arrival of the detectives. The louder-than-usual sound also meant that the wind blew out of the south and had pulled the door out of someone's hand. The presence of Tanya and Miguel waiting together for their arrival threw the detectives off stride because, taking Miguel on his previous word of working from the outside to the inner circle of the relatives, they had planned to take on the Anglos up at the administration office. Jefferson covered himself by shaking first Tanya's hand and then Miguel's. MacDonald followed him, bidding a strained good morning to both of them.

After the coffee ritual, MacDonald began by addressing Tanya, formally. "Ms. Tom, you have my condolences for the tragic death of your brother and sister-in-law. You know," he paused here to mark a break in the direction of his thoughts, "you know that the only way to walk on level ground this morning is, I think, to get rid of a few bumps. You see, I had a problem yesterday. I don't mind telling you, it was terribly awkward when you did not identify yourself as Lodge's sister. At the same time, we knew who you were by virtue of your position as the Chapter secretary. Nor did Miguel help us on this point. So, why was that? Why haven't you, or Miguel for that matter, openly acknowledged who you are?" MacDonald brought himself toward the front of his chair.

"Would your knowledge of who I am have supported your theories?" It wasn't really a question for them but an opening for herself. "Of course not." The ensuing silence now gave Tanya the opportunity she needed to communicate the importance of her grandfather in the handling of Lodge's death. She let her eyes rest on Miguel and with a note of confidence and finality in her voice, she said, "Until my grandfather ends his prayers, Mr. MacDonald, Lodge's passing is still going on. Miguel understands Grandfather's judgment in the Indian way because, when he told my grandfather and me about Lodge and Katy's death on Monday morning, we both heard Grandfather say, 'I must know.' So when he 'knows,' then Lodge's death will be final." Her eyes shifted from Miguel to each of the detectives in turn to see, not if they understood her words, but if they respected them.

"This is another culture thing, isn't it?" It was Jefferson's turn. "Tanya, let me be honest. Yesterday, Miguel tried to help us understand some of the cultural implications in these deaths. For example, he referred to the bad blood at Lodge's place. Now, you give us something about your Grandfather determining Lodge's death, as if it were a process, an ongoing event, and not an absolute bloody fact. Even more, you are saying that he might know who…" Jefferson felt yesterday's disgust rising in his throat.

"Look, I am trying to work with what, to me, are really, really difficult approaches to two terrible killings. These are some of the bumps that MacDonald talked about. In addition, Miguel, why did you change yesterday's strategy of interviewing the relatives last? See, your circles are still on the board over there. Jefferson kept the anger out of his voice and demeanor but, at the same time, he left no doubt that he was nearing the end of his wits.

Without looking up, Miguel started the explanation. But Tanya cut him off by easing her hand onto the table and waiting for both men to look at her. "It is just a matter of timing, gentlemen. As I have said, my grandfather is in a ceremonial Way that centers on his grandson's death, a death that has the evil implications of Bad Blood. Tonight, the ritual will end with a light on Horse Mountain. After that, I will be with him for two days. So, as a practical matter, and that is all that it is, it was I who changed Miguel's schedule. You can interview me either now or next week. Which do you prefer?"

MacDonald took charge, not wanting to touch the cultural reference again, and moved straight ahead. "Tanya, in your opinion, who killed Lodge and Katy?" Jefferson simply gazed at the floor, mentally afloat. Miguel began the snuff routine.

"I don't know. I believe that someone from outside of their home killed both of them. Lodge did not kill Katy and then himself. From what Miguel has described for me, moving bloody bodies and staging intercourse, there has been a desecration of the bodies. Such a way is not a Navajo way." For a moment, she put her two hands up in front of her, in a dismissal gesture. "No, no amount of rumor or police evidence will ever make me change my mind on that issue."

"What would be the motive? If you believe that it was a double murder, then why would someone do it? Why were they killed?" Jefferson purposely interrupted her thoughts, hoping for spontaneous answers that might give him something plausible.

As if a button had been pushed behind her defenseless eyes and with a very slight movement in the angle of her neck, Tanya shifted to the Anglos' sense of conversational timing: no more pauses, no waiting between answers. "Money," she whispered. "It is always about money."

"Had he spoken to you about the need for money?" Jefferson was getting somewhere; Tanya had just corroborated Pat Wade's story about money.

"Never. Never has he done so, nor would he ever. Such topics are not spoken of between a proud brother and his sister. Yet, everyone knows that the down payment for the new truck came from someone. This money brought with it a great deal of jealousy from his in-laws who, like all in-laws, resent extended family members who have good jobs and good connections. As a result, they are constantly finding ways to make people feel obligated to them so that they will give them money."

Miguel, up to this point, save for the snuff routine, had not so much as shifted in his chair during the interview. As if reading Jefferson's thoughts about Woodson's involvement in the report, he asked Tanya, "Do you think Woodson would kill them, for money, for anything?"

"Maybe out in the open, in the mountains, in their backs, from behind. But no, not in their house, and not in the housing project."

"Tell us, both of you, where do you think that he got the money for the truck?" Before Tanya could answer, Jefferson stood up, walked around behind his chair, and took a position from which he could observe both Miguel and Tanya and any interaction between them. He had to get rid of the nagging feeling that the two of them were setting him up.

"The School Board," she answered.

Miguel nodded. "Yes, that's right."

"So you both agree. Why? Was he a good friend of the board or its administration?"

Miguel spit a clop of black Copenhagen juice into his empty coffee cup, wiped his chin with the heel of his hand, which then flew to his armpit for a cleanup job. "Yes, you would think so. But the opposite is closer to the truth." Before he continued, he looked at Tanya for her permission. She gave it with a quick glance and then settled back, resigned for one more inevitable hurt.

Miguel continued, "In general, Lodge resented white people. One of them is his father, whom he had never met and who had never owned up to being his father. The school is another reason. White people come on the reservation and take 80 percent of all the money from the operation of the school—big salaries, bonuses, supplies, outlandish consultant contracts. Lodge kept telling the board that they were wrong, contracting for the white man's money but doing nothing to change the flow of the dollars to the Indian people, except for the members' own personal loans that they never pay back."

Miguel stopped, getting his thoughts in order, trying to separate his feelings from Lodge's, trying to keep his perspective as the Mexican cop. The two detectives recognized that Miguel, by putting the racial cards on the table, white man versus Indian, had put them in a box, at least temporarily. They gave him credit and remained silent.

Finally, Miguel continued. "And there is another reason that he didn't get on with the white administration. I couldn't agree with him more on this part. The Anglos use some of their big money for drugs and bring them here to the reservation. You see," Miguel was now Miguel, "every week, like a beat cop, I haul Navajos to the Battlefield Navajo jail and bring them to Navajo tribal court for drunkenness, DWI, and possession of alcohol. At the same time, the white people right next door in the same school housing complex where I arrest Navajos are getting stoned; and I can do nothing about it. How is that for justice, Mr. Washington officers?"

Both recognized that it wasn't a question but rather an emotional steamroller for the low- keyed Miguel. He hadn't finished.

"Do you know about Floyd Messenger?" Both detectives muttered that they did. "OK. Put the picture of his conviction of killing two old people in a vehicular homicide based on drug and alcohol charges right alongside another picture—a picture of a police dog from the Cuba County sheriff's office going into the Indian school up there and looking for drugs in the kids' lockers, but—now get this—never going near the administration building, where Mr. Messenger, the white man, sits stoned most of his day. Nor do they go near the Anglo homes where I know for a fact that drugs are stashed on their way through the reservation to other drug dealers. Why is it this way? Because the tribal politics allows only the school to be searched. Need I say more on how our local

Anglos manipulate the jurisdictional systems on Indian lands?"

"Miguel, are you saying that the deaths of Lodge and Katy are tied to drugs?" It was all MacDonald could do to keep his voice restrained and level, especially with the background that Tilden had provided earlier this morning at breakfast. He wanted to keep Miguel on this track.

"No," Miguel responded. The word was like a jackhammer to MacDonald's anticipation. His theory, or rather Tilden's, apparently did not fly with Miguel. "Those asshole druggies would do nothing—*nothing*—to jeopardize the good thing that they got going here on the reservation," Miguel said through clenched jaws. "On the other hand," Miguel paused. He wanted to say the next thing without hurting Tanya too deeply. "In my opinion, Lodge was so angry that he would not be above threatening his way into the Board's money or any Anglo money in whatever way he could."

Miguel's comment had partly verified Tilden's theory, in that there could be two levels of drug operations on the reservation: local users and, probably, local mules. Understanding what relating drugs to Lodge might be costing Tanya, Jefferson told her that the interview was over and asked her, as a manner of courtesy, if she wished to add anything.

She stood, looking directly at Miguel, and responded: "Lodge did not die because of his hatred for people or what they were doing. He died because someone hated him." As she walked out, Jefferson thought, *It was most interesting how Miguel protected Tanya by taking over her interview.*

CHAPTER 26

Saw Tooth Mountains
Wednesday

It was now too dark to use the scope. Under a cloudless sky, the afternoon drifted into evening and Robert, between eating jerky and dozing, had lain on his stomach the entire time. He was looking for signs of what had caused the poisoning of the overflow watering tank below. Nothing. Yet, he now could conclude a couple of things: First, if he were to find any answers to the activity below, he would have to do it in the dark. Whatever was operating down there would most certainly work only under the veil of darkness. Plodding into the area without the secrecy of night could cost him his life.

Secondly, something human had been below. Poisoning was an intentional act. Nature, alone, hardly ever allows poison into water. Water comes from 200 to 300 feet below ground and could never contain contaminants that could kill several large animals. Besides, the water in the tank, which had come directly from the pump, showed no signs of poisoning. Nothing was dead in the holding tank. Only the overflow basin from the tank showed death.

Thirdly, there had been no rain recently. Therefore, runoff could not have washed in surface poisons from the drainage areas. Man was the answer. Someone had placed poison in the pond, the venom of death.

Who was down there? A man who had now gone? Or a man who was now hidden, hunting and watching, like him, for him? In a way, it was reassuring because if there was a rifle-scope somewhere in the valley, it had not as yet found him. But what about a night scope? Robert was pretty sure that poison and a night scope would not be connected—high tech and low tech. Most importantly, if the deaths below were connected to Lodge and Katy, as Grandfather believed, neither of those killings was aided by the use a scope. In either case, it was apparent that the killer wanted his deeds to be public. But when and how did all of the destruction below take place?

Robert's thoughts ran on. *Let's suppose that I do find someone down there. Who could it be? A paramilitary jarhead?* He had heard that a ranch down in the San Juan Mountains was purchased recently by a retired general from West Virginia. That possibility could put a night scope over there on Horse Mountain.

Wait. Wait. Starting from the beginning again, he knew that he was out here in the first place because of Grandfather, Milton, and Tanya. A religious experience led by Grandfather as the result of the deaths of Lodge and Katy had now brought him face to face with more death and even the possibility of his own death. Grandfather had used religion to connect the two, the deaths in Lodge's house and the deaths in this canyon.

The deaths of people and animals meant that a man was involved, for sure. Religion added the possibility that more than a man could be behind these events. "Find it. Kill it. Burn it." The Bible stories flashed through his mind. Was Robert set up to put somebody on an altar? Or was he to be the sacrifice on someone else's altar? How could all of this religious stuff from the past pertain to today? Oh for god's sake, he had to hold it, hold it. Let someone else put all of that faith stuff together later.

Whoever or whatever is down there, if it was any good as a hunter, it would soon realize that it was the hunted. If it wanted to make me the hunted, it had better be pretty damn good.

Carefully, he put himself and his hunting gear together. This time, he wore his moccasins on and tied to his shoes to his backpack. Mentally he checked on the rest of his equipment, reassuring himself by touching each piece and visualizing its immediate use. Ready. Quietly, he walked north until he found the saddle he had used earlier and gently let himself over the crest.

This time Robert went to the Horse Mountain side, the death side, but hopefully, not his. Slowly, he worked his way south and at an angle of gradual descent so that he would be about a half mile below the windmill when he reached the canyon floor. It should take him about two hours and leave plenty of time to find his prey.

Now, he was Robert Sedillo. He moved carefully, making sure he was not exposed to the line of sight from the western slope of Horse Mountain. The only light came from the stars. The only noise came from his heartbeat. The movement of air was at his back. A deer in front of him confirmed this when it spooked and dashed on up to the crest soundlessly except for the faint rustle of leaves. He trusted himself to the shadows, as imperceptible as they might be. In doing so, he read any threats lurking in them. Finally, he was at the bottom, very close to the midnight hour.

After a few moments, he crossed over to the Horse Mountain side of the valley. The movement of air was in his face now, and the flow of his own scent was safely below him. Slowly, he began his gradual ascent on the slope of Horse Mountain. He eventually moved into a position above the water tank and hopefully above anything or anyone that was close to the tank. Twice within the next hour, he stopped, thinking that he had heard the beat of a drum. The first instance he discarded as his imagination.

The second time he heard it, he felt the beat was associated with his movements, as if the drum sound was in sync with his footsteps. The sound was playing with his mind; and as he realized it, the bowstring leapt up to his cheek, in a reflexive action. In a drawn position, he swept the area in a slow, circular motion, looking for a target. Nothing. Relaxing, he dropped to one knee and remained there without motion; drawing on every instinct to locate the source of the drum.

His reflections told him that the beat was from a ceremonial drum, the kind used to accompany a singer, not a dancer. But he could not distinguish a voice. He would wait. A fire would follow if this drumbeat were associated with a religious rite. Grandfather, Milton, and Tanya, with their ritual, had prepared him for this moment. They knew that the hunt that began as a religious ceremony in the Hogan, associated with Lodge and Katy's death, would somehow continue on the mountain. More death would be in this religious context and in the spirit of his father, John Sedillo. In acting it out, he would assure the safety of the people and signify it with a fire on Horse Mountain for the people to see and take comfort in. John Sedillo was present.

But were his movements being communicated to the drummer? First, he had to find out if that was the case and if so, how he was giving himself away. Slowly, Robert lowered the pack from his back. He removed one piece of rope from his belt and tied it to the arm strap of the pack. Then, lying on the ground, he crawled downward on his stomach. No drum. It took about ten minutes of belly crawling and pulling the backpack after him in silent inches until he found what he was looking for, a small outcropping of rocks that would allow him to lower the back pack over the edge. It worked.

About eight feet of the rope was out when the drum started again. This time he got its direction and stopped the rope. The drum stopped. The drummer was below him and between him and the poisoned drinking areas. He lowered the pack again, and the drum continued until the pack reached the ground and stopped. Robert let the rope drop down to the pack. Hopefully, his enemy will continue to confuse Robert's location with that of the back pack.

This uncanny detection of movement had him on the point of panic when he picked up the first traces of smoke. He waited, more smoke but no light from a fire. Still more smoke. Finally, it hit him that the smoke was the purpose of the fire, not the fire itself. Smoke to disorient Robert's own sense of smell, a Wall of Smoke to allow the spirits of the people to pass through, in this case, the evil ones.

Silently, he straightened up from his prone position and hung his bow over the end of a broken branch between him and the sound below. Without any decision and solely on instinct he pulled himself up into the tree. His movements were like those of a snake, in that he had one motion from branch to branch until he was high enough to see the source of the smoke and the flicker of a reflected light from the fire hidden behind a boulder. He froze, straining to bring his vision into focus on the location of the fire. There was no movement except that of the smoke curling up from its origin below the large stones. There, in the middle of the milky haze, a shadowy form became visible, silhouetted against the smoke moving around and above it. The inky glob even appeared to be suspended, but that fact was lost in the certainty that all of this was a baited trap. Drum, smoke, fire, images, all beckoned his attention; all were intended to force a response that could possibly mean his death.

CHAPTER 27

Lodge's office trailer
Wednesday morning

The first and second interviews of the day, Tilden's in Saw Tooth and now Tanya's on the reservation, had placed drugs at the heart of the investigation. Yet, for all of the discussion about drugs, no one person had been tied to the killings. After the interview with Tanya, Miguel told MacDonald and Jefferson that all of the Anglos from the School Board's administration would assemble in one of the classrooms at noon. With an hour to wait, the detectives decided to accept Wade's invitation of last night. They took their roast beef sandwiches over to the vocational-education trailer. Besides, they might look into Lodge's office for any insights into the deaths. The trailer idea for lunch was a mistake.

The trailer that housed Wade's adult-education programs for the Twin Rivers Navajo School Board, Inc. was a health hazard of unequaled proportions. Walls within the trailer had been moved to meet the various administrative needs over the past twenty years. The result was that floor registers for air circulation that once had abutted interior walls now lay in the middle of rooms or at the entryway to the main door.

As students and members of the community came into the building, the registers collected the shit from cattle corrals, the dung from sheep stalls, and whatever else could cling to boots. When the fan kicked in to heat or cool the rooms, the air was infused with a terrible odor, accompanied by particles of the collected bacteria. After Wade explained these facts about the atmosphere to his visitors, they each took a Coke from the icebox and a steel chair from his office and went outside to the shaded side of the trailer.

"It is good of you boys to take me up on my invitation." It was the same Wade who had joked with them last night. "From the looks of you, you also took my advice and got some supper rather than close the Cow Hide. Drinking your supper never helps the next day."

"No. No. We were good boys," MacDonald acknowledged. "Lodge's office is in this trailer, isn't it?" It was a statement more than a question. "As far as you know, has any of the family been around to look in or take anything?"

"Lodge was a private guy. Kept it locked. Did you notice that none of the doors in the trailer has a door set? These old house trailers were made that way, just clips to keep the door closed, but never locked. Now, if you wanted to lock your office, you had to put a clasp and padlock on it. Lodge did that. It hasn't been opened since he left last Friday afternoon. Now, I don't have a key. Don't suppose anyone does." Pat paused, waiting to see what reaction this would bring from the detectives.

Jefferson's mind tabulated all of the legal steps that should be followed in order to search Lodge's office. He placed that list of procedures against the absence of civil law in this isolated land of Twin Rivers. "Mr. Wade, get one of your students to run down Miguel and bring him over here, will you?"

Wade left and in a moment, the roar of a pickup truck confirmed that a student had gone in search of Miguel. "When Miguel gets here, we are going into Lodge's office. The question is simply how. The reason for Miguel's presence is merely for the record." MacDonald made the decision as the senior federal officer at the scene of a crime. And for a number of reasons, the whole reservation was the scene of this crime.

Within moments of Wade's return, Miguel came walking around the trailer. "One of Mr. Wade's students told me that you wanted to look into Lodge's office. I came by Tuesday and found it locked. Do you want to try the window or put a bolt cutter on the padlock?"

Wade provided the biggest bolt cutter that Jefferson had ever seen. It had enough leverage to make the Masters lock seem like a toy as it pressed its way through the hardened steel. When they entered the room, no one touched a thing. They moved in unison, the four pair of eyes trying to find something out of place in the eight-foot-by-eight-foot room. An old steel government-surplus desk from the 1940s faced one wall. Shelves on the wall opposite the desk contained nothing but a layer of dust. Jefferson opened the drawers of the desk with Wade looking over his shoulder. "Pat, do you see anything unusual in here or any place?"

"Just the same stuff as always. Wire pliers over there, saddle under the shelves, post hole digger in the corner. Lodge loved to walk the fence lines and repair them. That suitcase between the wall and the desk down there is new to me. I have never seen it before."

Jefferson put on gloves, picked it up, and placed it on the desk. It was a conventional, lightweight, aluminum suitcase, something that a field engineer might use to protect his equipment. There was no locking mechanism, and the clasp easily opened to reveal nothing. The unusual thing, though, was the handle. A brilliant, customized medallion hung from it. An eagle was etched in the center and outlined with expensive leather. "Miguel, how about you taking it over to Tanya and see if she can give you any ideas about it. Use these gloves, and don't let her touch it," Jefferson said. "Are the administrators waiting for us?"

Miguel told the detectives that he would meet them at the school in fifteen or twenty minutes. On the way out, he asked, "Mr. Wade, would you show them where the school conference room is located?" Jefferson and MacDonald walked out to their car and waited for Wade.

"Miguel, come by the classroom with me, will you?" Wade said. "Maybe the students can tell us something. Even though the rest of the school is out, the ranch's work goes on." He led Miguel down the hallway past the bathroom that had not been flushed in the past eight months. The floor was spongy under their footsteps because, over the years, the leak in the lavatory drain had rotted the joist under the floor. Laughter in the room quieted down as they entered the classroom. "Anyone ever seen this before?" Wade gestured at the aluminum suitcase. The eight young men in his range management class did not move a muscle, looked at no one, and placed all of their attention on their hats, thumbnails, or on spots on the table or the ceiling.

Wade expected as much and was unconcerned by the silence. But it did not mean that they knew nothing. Unlike Anglos, whose conversation inductively leads them somewhere; the Navajos must have the conclusion before they speak. "You know that the police are investigating the death of Lodge and Katy. The two men I had lunch with are BIA and FBI police officers. We just cut the padlock to Lodge's office. That suitcase in Officer Alonzo's hands was in there by his desk. I have never seen it before. Maybe Lodge purchased it to carry tools in. Do you know anything about it?"

More silence. Then one of them said something in Navajo for Miguel's benefit. Miguel answered, "This last Thursday?" Then, in English, "Do you mean that he found it on the

Petterson ranch or that he brought it out to the Peterson ranch last Thursday?"

The oldest student in the class took the lead. "It was not with us on the way to the ranch. He came back to where we work with it, about 10 a.m., after he checked the fence line between the Petterson ranch and Horse Mountain. Heavy, it no bounce in the truck. After lunch he drove off with it and then came back to pick us up about 5 p.m. Later, when we got back to the trailer, he took it into his office. Lighter, empty, this time." More silence. There was a final word in Navajo from one of the students. Miguel walked over to the table, wrote for a moment, and then each of the students signed the single sheet of paper with Miguel's writing on it. Mr. Wade watched it all and followed him out of the room, telling the students to go home for the day.

"Mr. Wade, go with the white folks up to the conference room in the school. I'll see you up there after touching base with Tanya. Interesting," he continued. "The students said Lodge believed that the suitcase belonged to Cornell Sussman, the Board's executive director."

CHAPTER 28

School conference room
Wednesday afternoon

Usually, the school's conference room gave newcomers the impression that an earthquake was in progress. It was no different for Jefferson and MacDonald. As they walked through the door, both stopped, prepared to turn and run, as they caught sight of a crack that ran up the wall in the far corner. About one inch wide at the floor, it gaped two or more inches near the ceiling. A stack of test papers reached halfway to the ceiling, adding to one's sense of instability in the fractured room.

"The engineer says that we are perfectly safe. The building is eight years old and has settled somewhat. I'm Cornell Sussman, the executive director of the Twin Rivers Navajo School Board, Inc." He shook their hands. Then he introduced Rhonda Fleming, Ben Tate, and Weldon Prince, to the federal officers.

A quality oak oblong table in the small room contrasted with the rusty, government-surplus steel chairs. The four administrators feathered together like a bird's tail at the far end of the table. Strangely, Wade did not join them but seated himself between the detectives and the administrators. As if on cue, when Tate sat down, the stack of test papers began to slide to the floor, one at a time. Embarrassed, the principal patiently counted them until they stopped.

Miguel's earlier depiction of the drug scene among the Anglos on the reservation brought Jefferson to his opening question. "Where is Floyd Messenger? Wasn't he informed of this meeting by Officer Alonzo?"

"Yes, sir, he was. Unfortunately, he had a doctor's appointment scheduled in Albuquerque this morning. He will be available tomorrow." Rhonda, as secretary, had a lot of experience in lying for the administration. Last night, at Sussman's direction, she'd made an appointment for him with a Western health doctor. "Would you like to make arrangements to interview him tomorrow?" she asked.

"Yes. At the same time, I would also like to see the loan papers for Lodge's truck. As you may know, people have been killed for a lot less. My information is correct, is it not, that Lodge obtained a loan for the down payment on the truck through your business office?" As he spoke, Jefferson's eyebrows furrowed in a manner that told Rhonda she had better be truthful in her reply.

"That is correct." It was Sussman who answered. "But the only loan paper is a resolution of the School Board approving the release of the money and accepting a schedule of salary deductions on his payroll account. Tribal sovereignty allows for a great deal of latitude in these matters."

Ignoring the sovereignty reference, Jefferson continued. "It's just my guess, but it seems to me that the Board has a bad loan right about now. Would you agree?" Evidence of rising blood pressure began to appear in the vein on the side of Sussman's jaw. Jefferson continued to be the bad guy. Swallowing his sarcasm, he said, "Tell us. How does a government institution make loans and cover bad debts like Lodge's? Do you have collateral or the title for the truck or, perhaps, a special slush account?" Jefferson still had the picture of Mrs. Tilden in his mind's eye.

"I am sure that the Board will handle it," Sussman replied. His real answer, one he could not tell the federal detectives was, in fact, quite simple. Lodge and Katy may be dead in Albuquerque but they would be dead in the payroll department when he said so. Their payroll checks would be deposited in the special account until the loan was repaid in full, with interest. Additionally, Sussman's position as a consultant to McGingle and Jones, the School Board's auditors, insured that such decisions were never questioned.

MacDonald continued the interview after Jefferson had made his point about the administrators playing with government money. "It's not that we are looking at any of you as murder suspects. However, it might be that the money and the truck could be tied to the motive for the killings of Lodge and Katy. By the way, it is true, is it not, that none of you were on the reservation Sunday night and early Monday morning? Correct?" MacDonald looked at Sussman, then Tate, then Prince, and then Rhonda as each confirmed that he or she was not on the reservation when the killings took place. Jefferson made notes as they described where they were and who could verify that information.

"All right, each of these alibis will be checked. Do any of you have anything to add to the remarks that you made to Miguel Alonzo on Monday about Lodge and Katy, remarks that would be helpful to this investigation?"

"Lodge and Katy thought that they were better than the other Navajos, owning things like their new truck. They were kind of a new middle class growing up on the reservation," Rhonda said. "They were difficult employees, always questioning directions or program procedures. Not generally liked by other Indians." Rhonda's remarks had been Sussman's idea. It was an effort to keep the suspicions on the reservation and away from the non-Indians.

Jefferson's mind raced to another conclusion. This time, he could not conceal his sarcasm. He said, "You mean, don't you, Rhonda, that you did not like them?" Jefferson found himself saying all the things that Alonzo had not been able to say over the years.

"What about any love triangles in either of their lives? Such stuff is good office gossip." As MacDonald asked, he looked over at Jefferson to give him the green light to follow up. Both Rhonda and Cornell looked at Prince to answer the question.

As he spoke, Prince hesitated just long enough to reveal a moment of weakness. "You could say that there were a lot of stories. I'm sure that your autopsy on Katy will reveal that she was pregnant. She came to the clinic for confirmation of this fact early last week. So I am not revealing anything new in this regard."

"You know Dan T., don't you, Dr. Prince?" Jefferson used the word "doctor" just to add to the uneasiness that any mention of Dan T. might cause him. "We interviewed him yesterday. He led us to believe that he worked with you, and that you could explain some information about Katy, information which both of you had. He said you could do a better job of explaining. Is his reference to the pregnancy? What else might he have meant?" Jefferson enjoyed what he did best: building an embarrassment beyond another's control.

The mere mention of Dan T.'s name yanked Prince's chain, but good. Sussman could not believe that Jefferson would know about the soreness in the Dan T./Prince relationship and how to use it so effectively. *That bastard is one dangerous person*, he thought.

"First, let me state that Dan T. is, effectively, an idiot from a brain injury that causes him to have delusions of grandeur." Prince kept a level, professional voice. "Now, the fact that Katy was pregnant is known. Any further information about

Katy, however, is privileged and I cannot discuss it." Prince believed that he had them on the doctor-patient relationship.

With a nod from Jefferson, Mr. Wade got up and left the room. In silence, everyone followed the echo of his footsteps to the front door, heard the door rattle, and then click open. Then they heard two or more sets of footsteps returning to the conference room. Never in his life had Weldon Prince felt such an urge to kill. He knew who was about to walk through the door. With his appearance, all of his well-crafted responses would melt away. The pounding in his head made him want to scream. Without looking up, Prince placed his hands on his knees and pressed his bent knuckles into the bottom of the table, hoping that the pain would clear his mind of fear and hatred. Whatever happens in the next five minutes of confusion, Prince must not make a reference to the Mexican doctor.

Dan T. , a newcomer to the meeting, entered the room with Mr. Wade and officer Alonzo. Dan T. walked over to the table and sat in an empty chair directly opposite Weldon Prince.

"All right," Prince began, "I see where I am." The pain had worked. Looking right into Dan T.'s eyes, he continued. "Dan T. must have overheard my conversation with Katy about...not wanting the pregnancy and...asking for an appointment in Albuquerque...concerning the termination of the pregnancy."

MacDonald held up his hand to give Prince some time before he answered the next question. "Are you suggesting that the baby was not her husband's?"

The arm dropped and Prince spoke with finality. "Yes."

"Anything else?"

Prince's self-control, like the tide going out, was slowly ebbing away. He reached for help in the depths of his hatred for the little man opposite him. "Yes, there is also the rumor, again one that is attributed to Dan T. here, a rumor that there was something between Katy Tom and me, and that I was the father of her unborn child." The words came out haltingly but loudly because, in truth, he wanted to shout, *"All because of this one stupid shit-head Indian!*

"All right, before I summarize what you are saying, let's ask Dan T. if he thought that Lodge Tom was aware—" Jefferson was cut off not so much by Miguel's effort to find a chair, but with the sudden appearance of an aluminum suitcase bouncing down the table toward Cornell at the other end. The medallion on the suitcase, like a claw protruding from a cat's paw, made a two-foot-long scratch in the middle of the table.

Startled, everyone threw his hands up and complained with different degrees of cursing, including Pat Wade, who yelped as he pushed back from the table, knocking over his steel chair. "So, Miguel, you got our attention. What the hell are you going to do with it?"

The ensuing confusion and banging of chairs saved Weldon Prince for a number of reasons. First, no one could distinguish his cry of shock at seeing one of Dr. Alquire's aluminum cases from the shouts of surprise and anger coming from the others. Secondly, because of the confusion, the detectives shifted their attention away from him and Katy's pregnancy.

"Actually, the case slipped out of my hand right about here after I hit the corner of the table. I'm sorry," Miguel said in an apologizing tone. "But it landed in the right place. Lodge said that it belonged to you, Cornell." Prince could not believe his luck.

Miguel, standing at the head of the table, held Cornell's gaze. Neither blinked, moved, or, it seemed, breathed. So far, the meeting had gone superbly well for Cornell, who had said nothing and pushed the attention away from himself and into other people's courts, especially Prince's. But now this goddam Miguel had put some serious business in his lap, literally.

"I don't know what the fuck you're talking about, Miguel." Standing up, he pushed the suitcase back up the table and moved around the chairs, toward Miguel. As the suitcase slid toward Miguel, Dan T. brought his knife down, handle first, onto the table with a terrible, vicious thud, right in front of Weldon Prince. The suitcase bounced off the knife and came to rest right in Prince's grasp. Dan T. spoke only so Prince could hear, "The Mexican is gone."

Everyone froze in the ensuing silence; their eyes on the knife. Sussman fell back into his chair. The detectives had their hands inside their coats. Dan T., in a very slow, deliberate motion, returned the knife to its sheath under his jacket, never taking his eyes off Prince. In a soft voice, Dan T. said, "Mr. Sussman, you have not answered Officer Alonzo's question."

"What do you say that we take five minutes? Mr. Wade, would you get the cokes that I set outside the door?" Wade responded immediately to Miguel's request. The excitement settled down with s few nervous laughs joining the rattling chairs and the popping of coke cans. But the heat was still in Sussman when things resumed.

"Officer Alonzo, the students, and you, too, Dan T., can all go to hell," Sussman spoke through clinched teeth.

To further irritate Sussman, MacDonald said, "I take it that that statement means no, the suitcase is not yours."

As if he had seen Dan T. like this every day, Alonzo followed up. "This piece of paper, Cornell, right here, has eight signatures verifying a statement that Lodge's last words ever spoken to his students were, 'The suitcase belongs to Cornell Sussman.'"

"It is not mine. With that I have no more to say," Cornell muttered.

Jefferson picked upon MacDonald's comment. "Cornell, do you have an opinion as to whom it might belong?" "Absolutely none." Cornell responded. Jefferson followed up, "Would anyone venture a guess as to where it came from or to whom it might belong?" Jefferson's question was met with absolute silence. "I guess that the students remain our only lead," Jefferson concluded.

When the knife had come down, only Weldon Prince had caught the flash of death in the weird eyes of Dan T. The message of the knife's impact and the deflection of the suitcase towards him were clear. *Dan T. knew about the connection between Prince and the suitcase and the Mexican. Could Dan T. be one of Alquire's Indians?* A cold sweat began to crawl like insects over his entire body. *Who else among the reservation's Indians belonged to Alquire's Indian network?* There would be absolutely no way of knowing. Prince resolved that if he ever got out of this room, he would never, ever, return to the Twin Rivers. Dr. Alquire, and, not least, Dan T.'s desire to kill him—all of it would be history.

CHAPTER 29

Three Mountain Top
Wednesday afternoon

*A*nd now it is time for the closest thing that we have to an *eyewitness, Woodson Pino,* thought Jefferson as he and MacDonald walked to the Chapter House.

"Mac, let's get Woodson Pino to spill his guts, tell us that he did it, and then let's get the hell out of here." Although Jefferson had taken a certain satisfaction in seeing those Anglos up at the school sweat, at most, they could only be indirectly involved in the actual killings. He continued, "And what the hell was Miguel thinking with the suitcase? I think Prince is right: Dan T. is a fucking fruitcake. What did Dan T. mutter to Prince when he plunged that knife in front of him? His voice is so high-pitched, anyway." MacDonald heard Jefferson's voice but was not listening to his words. They sounded just like more steam.

Miguel was waiting in the delegate's office. As they entered, he stood up, backed up to the wall, and put up his hands high in the air as if in total surrender. "I did it. I actually threw the suitcase at Sussman. I plead guilty. It was an accident that really did what I wanted it to do. Sussman was totally baffled. He did not know from nothing what was going on with the suitcase. His lack of recognition, at least for now in my judgment, cleared him. Do you agree? But, I am not sorry that I left him hanging on Lodge's last words."

233

"Agreed. Cornell has no direct connection with the suitcase. But, what is it with the note?" MacDonald took a sip of the coffee that was left over from early that morning and made a face. *The coffee is a bust*, he thought, *but at least the Chapter's office furniture is a lot more comfortable than those steel chairs up at the school.*

Miguel explained that he got the note from Mr. Wade's class after the two detectives had left. "It is for real. And, whether we like it or not, Lodge thought Cornell Sussman was involved with that suitcase." Miguel told them where it was found, namely, on Horse Mountain, but decided not to mention, for now, the students' story about the change in the weight of the suitcase. He would wait until some testing was done. "You people take this to your lab, will you?"

"Even though I don't think they're there, what if there are some fingerprints on the inside that match Sussman's prints, which, thanks to my detective work, are now on the outside? And by the way, Jefferson, what did you and MacDonald think of Dan T.'s act? He scared the hell out of everyone, didn't he? Most of all, Weldon Prince." That did it. Miguel finally brought a smile to Jefferson's face.

Unknown to Miguel in his moment of lightheartedness—and unfortunately for Weldon Prince—Dan T.'s little caper at the meeting had presented a reason for Prince's fingerprints to be on the suitcase, as well.

"All right, Miguel, so much for that meeting for now. Let's get on with Woodson Pino." Jefferson stood up and started for the door. Mac was with him. Miguel did not move. "Hang on." He waved them back into their chairs. "First, help me clear something up. Can you bring out the pictures of Lodge's house? When I looked into the house, I thought I saw an empty closet; everything was on the floor. There, you see what I mean. And the back porch…This picture shows it, like a tornado went through. The house was ransacked in every location big enough to hold this." Miguel tapped the suitcase. "But why kill if you didn't find it?"

"Interesting theory, Miguel. We'll keep it up here," pointing to his head. "Now, onto the Pinos.'" Jefferson again made his move.

"As soon as the Pinos see the dust from my vehicle, Woodson is going to be out and over the hill. I know it. If you two are with me, he will stay in the hills. Now, with a posse we could round up his ass. I know that. But maybe before that happens, let me try this. Woodson's brother, Willow Jr., is down the hall. He's the maintenance man for the reservation. I'll get him, and we'll go out to the Pinos in his truck. I am going to arrest Woodson for his own protection and bring him in for interrogation. In these circumstances, you'll have to agree, it is good, sound police practice."

"Do we wait here?" MacDonald looked at the top of Miguel's head as he bent over to put a large clop of Copenhagen into another white plastic cup. The hand and arm pit followed. The very essence of uncouthness, MacDonald thought.

"No. How about we meet you where we had lunch yesterday?"

Willow was dumbfounded when Miguel came into his office and told him that they were going out to Willow Sr.'s in Junior's pickup. After he had settled down, they pulled out of the Chapter compound and headed up to the turnoff to the Pinos' place. Woodson would be mad as hell, having been tricked into staying at home because Miguel was using Willow Jr.'s truck. As soon as they stopped in front of the Hogan and before the old man could protest, Miguel catapulted through the front door, found Woodson sleeping, and handcuffed him to the bed. Woodson's total passivity did not surprise Miguel; it confirmed his understanding of the people.

Then he walked back outside to the screams and shouts of the entire clan, who were gathering from every house in the compound. Miguel let them get their anger out. When it had subsided somewhat, Willow Jr. told the family what Miguel had instructed him to say: Woodson was under arrest for his own good.

First, there were threats against him in the community. Moreover, the detectives did not believe Woodson's story about bad blood. Rather, they thought Woodson either saw who did it and is lying to cover up for somebody, or he committed the murders himself and was seeking a cover for himself. Whatever the case, Woodson would be in custody either in Albuquerque or Cuba county jail for a few days.

Miguel told Willow Jr. to go into the Hogan and tell Woodson what was happening. The family followed him in and they talked together for about an hour. When they seemed satisfied, Miguel assured them that the brothers would stay together until Woodson came home. He hoped that they understood that Woodson had to be available for the next couple of days and that Willow Jr. would do all of the translating for him whenever they talked to the white man.

"Willow, here is the key for the handcuffs. Go unlock Woodson from the bed and put it on your wrist. I'll drive back." Total silence accompanied the two men from the Hogan to the truck. The family's stoic expressions conveyed more than just the willingness to endure the humiliation at having a family member arrested. They were judging Woodson for some additional reason. Miguel recognized the cultural undercurrent for what it was, but he had no way of knowing what was actually going on. For now, Miguel stored that feeling in his back pocket.

Willow Sr. had the final word. "Thank you for no red lights on my land. Here are Woodson's clothes." The old man handed Miguel a bag of clothes. *He doesn't miss much,* thought Miguel.

Woodson's face remained stone like until Miguel pulled off the blacktop and up into the Three Mountain Top area. Both men expressed fears of the unknown with unmistakable body language. The area had the additional fear of death in it from Katy's first husband. It had the effect Miguel wanted. Next, he wanted them to know that he was on their side. "Do you want to talk to the detectives at the Chapter House where the whole reservation will know what's going on, or here where no one will know? Take off the cuffs."

Again, they understood Miguel's concern for their privacy and relaxed a little.

Jefferson and MacDonald were sitting in the same place as they had yesterday. They had concluded that Miguel could not have handled the circumstances of this interview more cleverly. Without having to explain a thing, the questioning got down to the essentials as soon as everyone had claimed a rock or a position on the ground.

"Woodson, again, tell us what you saw Monday morning at Lodge's." Willow Jr. picked up Jefferson's question and translated it, never looking at Woodson. Silence. A silence that Willow Jr. expected. Woodson just looked down at the ground that he was sitting on, his head between his legs and his arms on his knees. Miguel broke the silence to Willow Jr. with a demand in Navajo to explain what was going on with his brother. Maybe his intuition about the Indian thing would come out now. Holding off Jefferson and MacDonald, Miguel continued, "Look. Apparently, I missed something about Woodson up until now. It is good that we are out here in the open. No one will ever know. We can talk about it."

What the hell difference does that make? Jefferson thought.

Willow Jr. waited as long as he could, hoping that the white people would grow impatient, fight with Miguel, and leave or turn the subject elsewhere.

Finally, Willow Jr. said, "It's Grandfather Tom." With the mention of his name, Woodson pulled his knees a little tighter to himself. "Grandfather told him to say nothing."

Jefferson began to stand up. As he did so, he threw some small stones that he was rattling in his hand. "Jefferson, don't blow the next few moments. They are very important to Woodson." Miguel's words were not a command but a reminder about their previous conversations in which he warned them that they must keep their minds open to what was going on among the People in the reservation.

"Willow, when did Grandfather Tom tell him this?" Miguel saw some things coming together because of the way Grandfather had acted when he brought word of Lodge's death.

"It was at a prayer meeting with Grandfather," Willow Jr. said, providing the information that the family had agreed would be given to white men.

"Who else was there?" Miguel let the question float out, conversationally, rather than indicating he was investigating.

Willow Jr. tried to get Woodson's attention but there was no response. After a pause, he said, "My folks, Woodson, Milton, maybe Tanya, and somebody else."

"When was the meeting?" Miguel followed up, trying to get a fix on Grandfather's activities.

"Yesterday night in North Chapel." Willow Jr. let out a deep sigh and kept looking at Woodson, whose contorted features spelled pain.

"So, Woodson is following a medicine man's instruction to say nothing? Why, Willow? Why has Grandfather Tom silenced him? Has Woodson done something?" Miguel felt that maybe Woodson would talk under the protection of the reservation elder.

"We got him," Jefferson thought as he finally figured out what Miguel was trying to do.

Willow Jr. stood up, looked to the south at Horse Mountain, the symbol of the People's refuge. With a sigh of resignation that comes from knowing that everything has been done to keep it in the family, Willow Jr. whispered, "He sold Katy's horse blanket last week."

"Willow, who bought it? Who was it?" Silence. Miguel urged the response as carefully as he could. At the same time, he could not miss the uneasiness of the two detectives who once again knew that these proceedings were out of their element. They wanted this questioning to go in a whole different direction. But, as with Tanya, Grandfather Tom was again in control.

"All Woodson can remember is that it was an Apache from Mescalero."

Jefferson could hold off no longer and half-shouted his question at the maintenance man in the dirty, greasy, black hat. "Why? Why would Woodson sell a goddam horse blanket in the first place, and why Katy's blanket?"

"I can answer that for you," Miguel said. He took up Jefferson's question in an effort to keep Willow Jr. on his side. "Willow Jr. and Woodson's mother makes the best blankets on the reservation, double sided. Maybe sells eight or ten a year. Three to five hundred dollars for each one." Then, looking back to Willow, Miguel asked, "Why Katy's blanket, Willow?"

"I don't know. Maybe he needed money."

"All right, Willow, take Woodson and go get into the detective's car. Get the clothes bag out of the truck." Both Pinos looked at Miguel as though betrayed. "It'll be all right. You are headed for Cuba for a couple of days' rest." Walking over to MacDonald, Miguel asked him to take the two men to Saw Tooth. He had arranged with Tilden to take them on into the Cuba County jail for a couple of days.

MacDonald waited a moment, thinking about Willow Jr.'s responses, looking at Horse Mountain, honestly trying to empathize with the Pinos and the situation. He simply couldn't do it. "Miguel, look, is this it? You mean a medicine man has put a curse on Woodson for selling Katy's horse blanket and that that is going to keep him from answering any of our questions concerning what happened at Lodge's?" Jefferson had walked on down the road a little to find some breathing room.

Without answering the question, Miguel pleaded, "Mac, if we can understand what happened to Lodge and Katy before the killings, we might understand the killings. Remember, Woodson's first words to me were, 'Bad blood.' That means, as I told you, that relatives are involved in the killings. However, Woodson never thought at that time that he was the one involved. He thought bad blood because of what he saw leave the house, or, at least, what he thought he saw.

"Woodson, unknowingly I believe, brought himself and his family into the bad blood killings when he sold that blanket. He believes that the person who bought it, or somebody else with him, used the blanket in a ceremony leading up to Lodge and Katy's death. Whether you buy it or not, that fact is a heavy load for Woodson and the Pino family. Woodson feels that the killer will come back for him. That's one of the reasons why I am putting him in the Cuba jail. Listen, I think we are getting close to somebody outside of Lodge's house who might be connected to the killings. Remember the 'V' I showed you? Well, the Indian thing and the Anglo investigation might just be coming together in this instance."

"Miguel, you just go ahead, connect all of these 'outside' Indian facts to Lodge's house, and write it up for us. Until then, it is so much nonsense to me. But what is not nonsense is this fact that Grandfather Tom, Woodson, and the whole bunch of Indians out here, are putting a big balloon out there in the hope that we will fly away on it. Tell them it won't happen. On the contrary, in my opinion, they are obstructing justice." MacDonald tried to get Miguel's eyes. Failing to do so, he concluded, "The best thing you've done today is put Woodson where we can find him." MacDonald walked over to the car and hit the horn to get Jefferson's attention. They left for Saw Tooth with the two Pinos.

CHAPTER 30

Saw Tooth Motel
Wednesday night

The trip to Tilden's office with Woodson and Willow Jr. had the solemnity of a funeral procession. After this last encounter with Miguel, Jefferson had concluded that the investigation on the reservation couldn't be deader. As far as he was concerned, the two zombies in the back seat were perfect symbols of not only the investigation, but of the whole damn reservation. He had tried two or three times to start a conversation with Willow Jr. to no avail. "I don't understand what you are asking," Willow Jr. would reply in his newly halting English.

Bullshit, he didn't. How could he be an interpreter for Woodson and at the same time not understand what Jefferson was saying? If he needed to, he would get an official interpreter and pressure these two local boys. And MacDonald's silence meant that he did not want to talk in front of the Navajos. *That's all right; let it be dead. I am ready to bury the fucking thing, from beginning to end,* he thought.

True to his word to Miguel, Tilden was waiting for them at his office. "I can tell that you had another great day with Miguel and the people of Twin Rivers. Welcome to our world." He put Woodson and Willow Jr. in his car and headed for Cuba. It would be another two hours before his day was over.

"Let's check the motel for any messages and reports. Hopefully, the man from Albuquerque waited for us so he can take this suitcase back with him," MacDonald said, sighing with relief at seeing Tilden's lights disappear. "I've seen a lot, been to a lot of places, investigated under what I thought were the most trying circumstances you can imagine. But this Twin Rivers world…and Grandfather Tom…what is his shit anyway?"

The "run man" was in the lobby of the motel, if it could be called that. Off to the left was a dining room that hadn't served a meal in many years. Chairs were stacked on dirty tables and the dust on the floor recorded each time a person went into whatever was beyond the far wall. There had been no attempt to demonstrate a business atmosphere. A counter with a broken glass top displayed empty boxes of Snickers and Butterfingers. The cash register drawer was never closed because the mechanical apparatus was jarred up. It perennially displayed a $7.33 transaction for groceries. Jefferson thought, *I have been in here three times and I never noticed any of this.*

The run man was Lester Guter. "Lester, thanks for the envelope. Here, let me sign. OK. Here ,you sign for this suitcase. Run it for prints and any analysis that they think appropriate. The dead man, Lodge Tom, apparently found it on a ranch south of Twin Rivers and said it belonged to one of the Anglos who work on the reservation."

Guter took the plastic bag with the case in it and squeezed himself around a stack of mattresses that were leaning against the wall next to the door. He was out and gone.

Back in their room, MacDonald asked Jefferson to make a bet on what was in the reports.

"I'll tell you what is in these reports. These babies have our tickets out of here. I better be right, that's all," Jefferson replied as he began reading the Crime Scene Report while MacDonald read the Initial Autopsy Report.

"Verification of the woman's pregnancy," MacDonald muttered. "That opens the door to all of the motivations we picked up from the Anglo administrators. Listen," he continued, "Each body had received one bullet; the female through the abdomen and exiting the back; the male through the neck and exiting the top of his head. Preliminary tests show that no drugs were found in the bodies. That will take some of the pressure off of the Anglos."

"The crime scene boys found four 30-06 casings. Three of the four shells were fired from the crime scene gun, supposedly Lodge's gun," Jefferson read. He went on to summarize the portion of his report that related to what MacDonald was saying.

"So, the fourth casing, the Winchester, was one that was just lying around the house?" MacDonald put a spirit of hope in his question, knowing there would be a problem if the fourth shell showed the same firing time as the others had. After a moment of silence, as Jefferson finished that part of the report, he said, "Sorry, the four cartridges were fired in the same time frame, as near as they can determine."

"But, what the hell? There was no other gun found in the house. Was there?" As if answering his own question, MacDonald continued, "So we have to conclude that another gun was fired before the deaths of the victims."

"Not necessarily." Jefferson turned a page of the report over and drew two guns, one with a casing in it, and three casings outside of the guns, one of which he circled. "In the murder-suicide theory, the last shell fired, the one with the casing still in the gun, would be the suicide shot. The bullet would go out through the roof. This would verify the entry to Lodge's neck and the exit from the top of the head, assuming that he was sitting or standing." He drew an X through the casing in the gun. And yes the report speaks about a bullet hole in the ceiling and roof."

"Next, the bullet found in the wall…does it match either casing number one or number two from Lodge's gun? Yes." He read that portion of the report that identified the bullet found in the wall as having come from one of two shells that were fired from Lodge's gun and that were found on the floor. Jefferson then crossed out a second casing on the paper.

"From the position of Lodge's body we must conclude that somebody moved it. He could not have blown off his head and fallen on Katy in that manner. Nor could the gun have gotten to its position if there was a suicide shot from the present location of Lodge's body. Is there any way that we can tie the bullet found in the wall with Katy's death? If we cannot, there is a possibility that this circled shell and another gun killed Katy Tom.

"Because one body was moved, the other one could likewise have been moved." Both men tried to find the basis in the report that would refute that possibility. They traded reports and read and reread them, looking for that one angle. After another ten minutes, they set the reports down. Jefferson asked, "What is the logical conclusion?"

MacDonald answered, "Number one, Woodson or somebody else was in that room. Number two, another gun fired that shell in the circle. Woodson could have done it before he went for Miguel. He then walked across old lady Gonandonegro's yard and threw the gun across the fence. Somebody picked it up."

With the mention of grandma Ganandonegro's name, Jefferson jumped from the bed and bounded across the room to his notebook on the dresser. "Wait, just wait a moment. Hold everything right where it is at." He flipped through the pages. Moments later he raises his left arm with a finger pointing upwards and shouts, "Number one is right here." And a second later he whispers, "Number two. We have two witnesses, grandma and Dan T. who verify the fact that four shots were fired, two in the evening and two in the middle of the night. The reports mention nothing about cartridge's being found outside. So…even though the shots were fired outside, the empty shells were ejected from the gun inside of the house and thus accounts for the four mentioned in the report."

MacDonald responded, "I knew I brought you for a reason. That does it. We got Lodge shooting Katy and then himself. We have a visitor, possibly more, who rearranges the bodies and takes a gun. Agreed?"

MacDonald continues, "One of the visitors was Woodson. His boots would account for the match of the prints that Miguel found in the old lady's yard and the one on Lodge's front porch, forgetting for a moment, the report here says that the print could possibly have come from a very large canine-type animal."

Following Mac's reasoning, Jefferson concluded that Woodson could have shot Katy and then used Lodge's gun to blow Lodge's brains out through the roof. But what about the prints on Lodge's gun? Woodson's prints were not on the gun. And what about the amount of blood on Woodson's clothing when Miguel finally looked for it? Woodson's clothes in the bag sent to Albuquerque could not have been used to move those two bodies. Lastly, where is the physical evidence of Woodson in that room? Shit, it was late. He was tired, hungry, and eager to put an end to the day. There was more to learn from their future talks with Woodson.

They decided on beer from the Cow Hide and hamburgers from the Saw Tooth Café. Jefferson got the food and MacDonald went up the street after the beer. Since MacDonald had the shortest distance to travel for the beer, on his return, he opened one as he waited. When the hamburgers arrived, he was dragging furniture out of the room so that they could sit in the cool of the evening and eat supper.

Two hours later, after much discussion, they had concluded that the case at Twin Rivers was over for them, at least for a couple of days. They would give Miguel these reports tomorrow and be on their merry way. Nothing indicated that some third party was in the room before the deaths. Whoever came in, came in after they were dead. Murder, suicide, and a third party moved the bodies after the killings. That same somebody also turned out the lights. It all pointed to Woodson.

Towards midnight, Jefferson suddenly let his feet drop from the railing that enclosed the sidewalk around the motel. He directed MacDonald's attention to the strange glow in the sky out toward the Twin Rivers reservation. Both men ran to the front of the motel to get a clearer view. Cars were stopping in the middle of the highway and people standing up on their hoods and roofs in order to get their bearings on the fire. Jefferson, referencing Tanya's comment about the light on Horse Mountain, commented, "I know I have not been too kind to the Navajos up there. But whatever in hell that fire is all about, I really do hope that it is working for her."

CHAPTER 31

Robert eased onto the ground from the tree, every movement flowing with the efficiency and urgency of a trained soldier in mortal combat. The option of running up the canyon and over to Donkey Springs where Feather was waiting pulled for his attention. His thoughts and the mechanics of his hands, however, were carrying out the plan for his survival. That now included certain death for the hunted who, he now knew, was definitely more of a man than whatever else it might be. No more distractions now with people, Grandfather, or Lodge and Katy's deaths. None of it mattered without scoring a hit in the next ten minutes and saving his own life.

Robert's hand found what he was searching for with wide sweeps in the side pockets of his fatigue pants: his old Zippo lighter. As he unsnapped the casing around its handle, his knife leaped into his hand and began making a hole in the ground, about six inches deep. Anyone looking at him would, with his next move, gasp for fear of his innards. He put the knife under his T-shirt and ripped it downward, four times, making four tailings that he quickly cut off.

Detaching the lighter from its casing Robert next pulled the cotton from the Zippo. He put the lighter down with the cotton on the outside surface of the Zippo. It was right next to the four pieces of cloth from his T-shirt, all close to his left knee. Feeling the cotton on top of the lighter, he laid the knife across the cotton and cut it into three pieces. Without getting up, he reached around and flipped the bow off the tree limb. Quickly, he took three arrows out of the quiver and put them next to his right knee.

Sixty seconds could be the extent of his lifetime. If a bullet did not find him in those moments, it would not be he who would be served up in the conflagration that was to follow; it would be the hunted. Everything was ready. He took a piece of cloth, tied a section of the cotton from the Zippo in it and then wrapped the cloth around the broad head of his first arrow, squeezing the lighter fluid from the cotton into the strip of T-shirt. He repeated the process with the next two arrows. The drumming had begun again; and, as far as he could tell, it was still coming from the same direction.

The final step and the beginning of the end were now at hand. The lighter went back into its case and then into the bottom of the hole. He notched his first arrow, reached over, and flipped the wheel on the lighter. His location was given away the instant that the spark from the flint hit the wick. He laid the covered broad head into the flame and immediately it caught with a bluish flame that targeted his entire body within a circle of light.

Robert sent the flaming arrow out over the tops of the trees and down toward the drummer in an arc of startling beauty. Flames left the arrow as it plunged to the earth. As the arrow reached its apex, a rifle resounded, sending a bullet into a nearby tree with such a thud that it actually shook the ground; a 30-06 or bigger. Without waiting to see where the first arrow had landed and if it were still burning, Robert shot a second arrow, spewing flames into the darkness. This time it had lesser arc and was about thirty yards closer, up the side of the mountain. As the third arrow burned over the lighter, Robert pushed some dirt into the hole with his knee and extinguished the lighter's flame. The last burning arrow cut into the sky as the second rifle shot echoed in the hills. The bullet was closer, but this time, above him. As soon as the last arrow had left his bow, Robert raced down the hill toward his backpack.

He stopped just long enough to see if the fire in his arrows had caught. They had. His first arrow was moving a main line of fire upward in the grass, with a branch of it settling into a cedar bush. A second fire had caught about one third of the way up a pine tree, where the dead branches were igniting one after the other up toward the top of the tree. No sign of the third arrow.

All of this was a passing image. The sound of the next shot came from above him and he knew that his plan had worked. The fires had drawn the hunted toward them. The prey had run up the hill while Robert had run down the hill. Without thinking, the hunted had run from the only safe place that the flaming mountain could afford him.

His backpack was now almost visible from the light that the fires were generating. In stride, he grabbed it, slung the pack over his right shoulder, and broke in a dead run for the water tank. He heard no further shots. Robert knew that his adversary had to have realized by now that the fires that had pulled him up the side of the mountain were now encircling him and that his safety also lay below and likewise in the water tank. Robert reached the canyon floor and raced down toward the windmill, eerily visible in the night sky being licked by the tongues of fire. If he had calculated correctly, the hunted was racing down the mountain, the fire closing in on him, and the smoke from his own fire was in front of him. That smoke should shield Robert because the draft from the fire above would be pulling that smoke up the hill into the face of his adversary.

As the overflow tank came into view, a stench reached his olfactory system and caused him to gasp and stumble forward. His senses stayed with him, even though the abrasions on his legs and knees screamed in pain. Quickly regaining his feet, he pushed on toward the water tank, swiping the dirt from his face and at the same time trying to shield his nose from the hideous combination of decaying and burning flesh that came from the dead cow lying closest to the timberline. In all of it, he had not loosened his grasp on the bow. The moment of truth arrived as he reached the poisoned overflow tank, his moccasin feet nearly stepping into it.

He turned up toward the fire. There, running down towards him with the rifle held in front of him, came the racing burning figure of the hunted. Robert knew that the creature had not seen his enemy or Robert would be dead. The reason that Robert was not seen? The mountain's fire was now reflected in the poisoned water and buried his presence in its blurring image. Ironically, what had killed others, the poisoned water, was now saving Robert. Dropping to one knee just outside the overflow tank, he notched an arrow and brought the string to his cheek. Robert steadied himself, keeping the tip of the broad head on the target's head, automatically allowing for the fact that he was shooting up hill and the kill would be about sixty yards away when his prey broke through the Wall of Smoke.

Realizing too late that its antagonist had beaten it to the safety of the water, the creature, almost in slow motion floated through the Wall of Smoke at the same instant that an arrow pierced its chest. The angle of the arrow continued into its stomach, and, finally, exited about six inches above its right hip. As the creature tumbled forward, the wolf's skin flew up into the air and, now unattached, seemingly had a death of its own as it rolled into a burning brush. The rifle, arcing high into the air, cast a long shadow from the fire that was now roaring up and down the side of Horse Mountain. All of it, the creature, the skin, and the rifle, came to rest, accompanied by a man's terrible howl of agonizing pain in death, his blood flowing into the earth.

The heat of the fire broke Robert's trance, his arm still poised in perfect alignment with the source of the now diminishing screams of the hunted. Slowly, he crawled the final feet around the overflow pond and reached the wall of the water tank. In the daze that follows the use of the last traces of a person's adrenalin, he pitched the bow and backpack up into the tank. He stripped naked, except for the moccasins, leaving his clothes on the ground next to the tank, and pulled himself to the safety of the water. The four feet of water in the five-foot tank felt extremely cold compared to the temperature of the air around him. So intense was the fire that there were moments in the next few minutes when he felt that there was no air to breathe. The sides of the water tank began to register the heat. Gradually, the fire was over and beyond the tank. In its wake were bellows of rising smoke from glowing embers.

Robert did not move. After several minutes, he realized that he was in the middle of a large, expanding circle of flames that was growing mostly north and east up the side of Horse Mountain. It was moving westward as well, but at a much slower pace due to the prevailing wind. How could he get by it and down to Feather tethered at Donkey Springs? The thoughts of his horse tied and unable to move quickly from an encroaching fire pushed him up and over the tank's edge, dragging the back pack and bow into the charred dust on the ground.

Robert realized that the shimmer of light next to his foot was his belt buckle reflecting the light from the heavens of fire. It was all that was left of the clothing that he had thrown off. It amazed him that he had enough presence of mind to remember that he did not want to poison the water or himself in case any of his clothing touched the overflow tank. He kicked the buckle into the water and listened to it cool in the sizzling steam.

Reaching down to pick it up, he saw a water soaked saddle blanket had been thrown over the side of the water tank. The appearance of the blanket brought him back to the religious thing again. Everything was tied together with Grandfather, the Hogan, the spirits of his father's people, Lodge, Katy, and the Walls of Smoke, one in the Hogan and the other all around him. His shivering body told him that he must move or die.

Opening his backpack, he tossed the buckle in and pulled out his sopping plastic rain gear. It stuck to his wet skin and eventually warmed him. Pulling the riding blanket from the water tank he began to make his way up the burned-out and smoking arroyo, the safest way to the fence line and to Donkey Springs. *The first guy in here*, he thought, *will wonder how an Indian's moccasin suddenly appeared out of nowhere in the ashes of Horse Mountain.*

The thought of the dead creature, man or beast, did not enter his mind.

CHAPTER 32

Saw Tooth Mountains
Thursday morning

When the alarm had moved through the village of Saw Tooth, the streets had filled with people and trucks. All seemed to be either moving toward or away from the Forest Service district office on the main street. Soon, a snake of vehicle lights began moving up the road toward the growing light of fire in the sky. As they made their way, everyone began supposing what had happened on or near the reservation: what ranchers were involved; whose livestock was on what range; could they contain it; and when in hell were the fire teams from Albuquerque getting down here.

With the bluffs to the west and the prevailing wind from the west, the fire moved slowly up, over, and down the mountain that had been home to Robert during the first day of the hunt, completely wiping out any trace of his presence. The blaze then began to smolder out as it worked its way into the wet grassland of Donkey Springs and its runoff down the canyon.

The rangers from the Saw Tooth Forest Service's district office led the firefight on the south. A function of each district office is to train firefighting crews that become standby resources to fight fires throughout the entire Southwest. These crews were among the first on the road to Horse Mountain, within minutes of the first alert. They intended to put a wall between the fire and the town of Saw Tooth, twenty-five miles to the south. The best place for that was the area where earlier ranch-management projects below Horse Mountain had bulldozed large areas of pinion and cedar trees into long rows of brush every quarter of a mile. Beating back the grass fire between these brush lines was the main activity that soon brought the southern boundary of the fire under control.

The Indian people from the reservation responded to the fire almost immediately, principally because a great number, while never expecting a fire of this magnitude, were looking for a light on Horse Mountain. A steady stream of car and truck lights surrounded the north and east side of the mountain. Some of them took up locations along the only paved road into the reservation. It formed a cut through the east side of the fire. The people were on every ember that blew across the road.

The tallest trees near the fence line were pinion and cedar, not the giant pines that covered the top of the mountain. As a result, there were no crowning fires near the road. Nor was the heat as intense as it must have been in the pine trees. Although their task was not easy, they succeeded in keeping the blaze contained to the mountain side of the road.

On the reservation side of the mountain, there was only a grass fire once the blaze moved across the fence line. All of the pinion and cedar trees had long ago been cut from the Twin Rivers for construction of Hogans or for firewood that was used or sold off the reservation. Generations of over-grazing had removed 90 percent of the grass. Without any danger, then, the brush fires were easily contained.

By midday, the firefighters were on Horse Mountain, digging out areas of potential flare-ups and gradually working their way to the windmill up in the canyon. The first report of the moccasin tracks leading out of the canyon spread rapidly among the crews along the fire line. Some members of the Navajo crews grew anxious and traded positions with their white counterparts. The Navajos went to the hot spots on top of the mountain while non-Navajos descended to see the footsteps in the ashes of the arroyo. Eventually, the Forest Service rangers reached the area of the windmill and concluded that the fire had had its origin in this area, principally because of the relative coolness as compared to other locations.

When the burned-out rifle was found near what could possibly be the remains of a human being, the ranger reported to his base station asking for the appropriate assistance. Meanwhile, everybody was pulled back from the windmill area and the arroyo leading up into the reservation, preserving the path that the moccasin feet had apparently taken. A ranger remained in the area, waiting for the police and fire investigators.

Word of the remains found at the windmill traveled to everyone surrounding the mountain and eventually reached Miguel, who was working with the fire crews on the reservation side. He walked the mile back to his Suburban and contacted Tilden, who was already on his way to the reservation. "I've been trying to reach you, Chief. Look, I got the same story that the Indians reported to you. The ranger had reported to his district office and it was relayed to me. The state police are also aware. The traffic into the reservation is heavy and slow going, as you can imagine, with all of the firefighters and heavy equipment. Believe it or not, I am looking at MacDonald and Jefferson, waiting, along with me and a bunch of other people. A big old water tanker is just pulling its way out of Big Screw Canyon."

Miguel could hear some of the commotion that Tilden was describing over the radio. "Tilden, look for my truck about ten miles down the road from where you are. Once you get here, we'll go to Horse Mountain from the reservation side, up the arroyo to the windmill. Do you think that the dead person has any connection to the deaths of Lodge and Katy?"

Tilden replied, "I had the exact same question. Later..."

When they arrived about an hour later, Miguel was looking through a pair of field glasses at the arroyo that led back up into the canyon and the windmill. The Indian people had formed a line along the arroyo, starting about a quarter of a mile from the burned fence line. Each police officer in turn surveyed the same activity.

"If I am not mistaken, that is Dan T. walking toward the fence," Jefferson chuckled to himself. "No, no wait. He turned around now and is walking back toward the group of men. For sure, Dan T. wanted to go up to the windmill and see for himself. Apparently they are arguing with him."

Handing the glasses back to Miguel, Jefferson said, "Miguel, first, let me apologize. I know that I have spoken my mind about the Indian thing over the past couple of days. It seemed like it was just getting in the way of the real facts. But," Jefferson took his time, reaching inside of his coat for the reports. "Last night, MacDonald and I reached the same conclusion. Although there are some unanswered questions, these documents give us the solid ground to make the decision that Lodge killed Katy and then shot himself. We know that what we think about the investigation doesn't in the least solve your problems in the community. Add to the investigation this fire and, from what Tilden told us, another body up in the canyon over there, and well, there is just no way that we should be hanging around." Jefferson swung his arms out at the mountain smoldering like a single enormous cinder. "Look at Horse Mountain over there, smoking away, and the people from the reservation gathered at that arroyo..."

He stopped. "Miguel, we're out of here. We will be back in a couple of days."

MacDonald quickly added, "We have nothing yet on the suitcase. Like he said, the only reason that Jefferson and I came up here this morning was to deliver the reports and to tell you that we were leaving. Oh yes, the Pino boys are doing well in Cuba. We will hold on to them for a couple more days. Finally, I can't believe that you won't be glad that we're out of your hair." Both MacDonald and Jefferson chuckled a little, hoping to give Miguel an opening without really meeting the crux of the cultural problems in the investigation.

Miguel took the reports. "You know that grandfather Tom will never buy your conclusions, don't you? If he wishes, be prepared to talk with him. We will be in touch. Take care. Tilden, get your camera." Without another word, Miguel shook hands with the detectives and pushed Tilden towards his Suburban. Bidding them good-bye, Tilden grabbed the intertwined cords of his camera and canteen from the front seat of his truck.

Miguel slowly drove the truck across the reservation, sometimes following roads, other times staying in a straight line towards the arroyo. *The two detectives did the right thing in going away for a couple of days, at least. They don't belong loose on the reservation by themselves. And I cannot be with them right now,* he thought. *I was right last night. The two men could not listen and unemotionally separate the Navajo involvement in these deaths from their own perceptions of the investigation.* He knew how difficult it was. Only several very bad experiences had taught him. With these thoughts, he put MacDonald and Jefferson behind him.

Slowly, Jefferson and MacDonald drove back to Saw Tooth amid the steady pouring of smoke across the road.

The cattle guard to the reservation, once again and for the last time, drummed its final farewell beat at them. They knew that Twin Rivers was over for them, for good.

They couldn't have been more wrong.

CHAPTER 33

Saw Tooth Mountains
Thursday afternoon

As soon as the people recognized that Miguel was coming towards them in the police van, they began moving
away, leaving Dan T. standing alone.

"All right, Dan T.," Miguel said with the inflection of an
invitation.

"Come here, I'll show you." Dan T. and the officers
walked until they entered the burned area on the reservation
side. Then he led them to the arroyo, down from the fence
line about a quarter of a mile. It offered them a view both up
and down the arroyo. Looking down, Miguel and Tilden saw
the clear moccasin footprints, apparently originating in the
canyon on Horse Mountain and continuing on toward the
crowd of Navajos below them.

"See where the people are scattered and looking all
around? That is where the fire ended and along with it the
moccasin's footprint. They want to follow it on the unburned
area but can find no trace of it, mostly because of their own
thrashing around in putting out the fire last night."

Tilden needed to let Dan T. know that Horse Mountain,
even though a sacred mountain to the tribe, was outside of
the reservation and on county property. His decisions were
the ones that were going to count now, not Miguel's. He said,
"Dan T., we have to say that someone walked out of that

canyon after the fire. The ranger is telling us that the prints go all the way back to the windmill. Apparently, the People know all about it. What do they say is going on?"

Dan T. looked at a silent Miguel. In Navajo, he said, "He won't understand, Miguel."

"Try him, Dan T.," were Miguel's only words. On schedule, the Copenhagen came out.

Taking his time, Dan T. began, "There are some powerful medicines among the People now. The fire, the tracks, Lodge and Katy's deaths, and maybe another dead man on the sacred mountain. Yes, we heard about it. The spirits of our people are visiting us. The People believe that the very sight of these tracks will protect them. That is why you see so many of them are coming and going. The fire and the footprints were the spirits' sign to us."

"That's fine with me. But I am going to follow those tracks back up the canyon and—"

Miguel did not so much interrupt Tilden as complete his sentence with his own train of thought. "And he needs your assistance, Dan T." Miguel continued, "Perhaps you will give us your protection, if not from the bad medicine, then from the People's misunderstanding of our intentions. Later, he may have to take a team of police up there, across the reservation. Also, I am sure that there are some fire investigators on their way in there from the other side. Do you understand what he is asking?"

Without another word, Dan T. walked down to the group of Navajos. Whatever he said, they all shook their heads in the same manner. He then took the lead in walking towards the fence line. Miguel purposely slowed Tilden until Dan T.'s lead demonstrated for the onlookers that he was in charge. "Thank you, Tilden," Miguel whispered.

When they reached the gate, Dan T. held up his hands for them to stop. Miguel's heart nearly came out of his chest when he saw what Dan T. was holding up in his hands for everyone to see. He was parading with it, or perhaps dancing with it, back and forth in the shadow of the Horse Mountain. It was a blanket, and sure as hell, the same blanket as described by Willow Jr. and sold by Woodson. It was Katy's horse blanket. How, in God's name…

The policeman in Miguel snapped him out of his amazement. He held out his hand for Tilden's camera. Without trying to untangle the camera and the canteen, Tilden gave them both to Miguel. "Go on over there and stand next to Dan T." Miguel took several pictures, a couple as close up as possible.

Without bringing Tilden in on the background of the blanket and what it meant to the Pino family, Miguel asked, "Dan T., any ideas?"

"Easy. The spirit whose tracks are below, in the arroyo, left it here. Our possession is the sign that the bad blood has turned itself against the evil spirits," Dan T. answered.

Yeah, and we all pissed out the fire last night. Tilden bit his lip so that he would not say it aloud.

Miguel, not knowing if Dan T. knew it was the Pinos' blanket, again said nothing. Yet he wondered, *What if he knows that he is holding the very thing that the Pinos believe put the curse on their daughter, the very thing that Woodson and apparently Grandfather Tom accepted as an instrument of death? Yet, he is holding it up like a damn trophy.* He felt the blanket as Dan T. put it back on the fence. It was damp, unmarred by the fire. It had to have been put there after the fire passed through. *What a contrast,* he thought. *Blackened fence posts, burned brush and trees, and hanging barbed wires holding a beautiful, expensive, gray horse blanket. It could have meaning only on the Twin Rivers Reservation.*

The trio crossed the reservation boundary and what was left of the fence line. Again, Dan T. was out in front, examining the moccasin tracks from above the arroyo until it flattened out in the wide windmill area. The main water drainage of the arroyo continued way off to the left, nearer the base of the mountain. Although the windmill was less than a quarter of a mile from the reservation, the change in terrain was that of pinion to pine. Where it was once a majestic green, offering its sweet shade from the hot sun, the area was now blackened, smoldering with wisps of smoke that stretched out to a clear, blue sky.

Out of this desolation, in the darkened, burned-out canyon, a call echoed down to them from above. "Is that you Tilden, Miguel? Stop right where you are for a moment." The forest ranger, Sam Perkins, carefully made his way down from the side of the hill until he stood next to them. "Even though it doesn't look like it from all of the trampling, we are trying to retain this area for the fire inspectors and the boys from the state crime lab. If you look, there are several paths around here.

"Once we realized what the hell we had, we tried to stay on those paths. I see that you recognized the path over to the reservation because you stayed away from the moccasin trail. The path to your left goes up to the remains of a body. There is a burned-out rifle about fifteen feet ahead and down from it. If you'll follow me, you'll see where the moccasin trail begins next to the windmill."

"Tilden, this is your world," Miguel said. "If it is all right, I am going to go over there, sit down in the ashes, and just take in this scene for a while. Dan T., since you are here in kind of an official capacity, inasmuch as you will be making a report to the People, what is it you want to do that will not disturb the area?"

"I wish to climb to the ridge from here up. The Twin Rivers people have many sites on the mountain, sweat lodges, ancient Hogans, burial sites. I will check some of them. OK with you, Ranger?"

The ranger took the moment to stress to Dan T., "It looks as though a murderer might have escaped last night into the reservation, a murderer with Indian shoes on." Turning to Miguel, he said, "Miguel, if I am right, in addition to Katy and Lodge, you have another big problem to attend to over there." Then returning to Dan T., he continued, "At this time, we have no idea where those feet came from; but they surely left after that…whatever it is over there…was dead. Be sure to include that in your report, as well. Now go ahead, but stay clear of those two areas over there."

Miguel and Dan T. left in opposite directions while Tilden and the ranger did their official thing. First, after clearing a place near a pile of rocks, Miguel sat, closed his eyes, and listened. Besides the mutterings of the two officers and Dan T. moving up the side of the mountain, there was the rattle of the windmill turning freely without any drag because the sucker rod had burned off and the leathers had dropped to the bottom of the pump. Then, he could distinguish nothing else. No rustling of leaves, needles, branches. No sounds of life below or above or in the trees. The movement of wind was the most unsettling. As it moved through the barren trees, tiny shrieks could be heard, once associated with ghosts.

He opened his eyes to watch Dan T. His thoughts again turned to Dan T.'s dancing with the blanket. If it was a sign of victory, then it was a symbol of this fire, a fire that was probably caused for a good reason. The destruction had achieved a victory over something, or someone, but who? The dead man over there? And for God's sake, why? Miguel could not figure Dan T.'s reference to the bad blood.

Miguel let his thoughts go backwards with the events associated with the so-called trophy. Dan T. celebrating a blanket and a fire; a blanket belonging to Katy Pino and sold by her brother, Woodson; a blanket for which Grandfather Tom cursed Woodson in a religious ceremony; a blanket, one of many, made by Katy's mother; a blanket purchased by an Apache, perhaps, a blanket used by Lodge and Katy on their horses. All of these people are now connected. Jefferson would surely go berserk with this train of thought.

Another thing: Did the blanket actually connect this place, this mountain, to Lodge and Katy's house, the place of their deaths? If it did, then the person with the moccasin feet and the person whose remains were lying over there could be part of Lodge and Katy's death scene, as well.

He looked over at the arroyo with the moccasin foot-prints. Who the hell went out of here? *Who are you? Do those charred remains over there have anything to do with you?* Is it just a coincidence that the fire connects the blanket, the remains, and the individual who escaped the fire? There are no coincidences. Apparent contradictions exist only because there are no explanations. Miguel knew that he would, at least for a time, have to live with a lot of questions, not the least of which was this one: *Grandfather Tom, how are you on this mountain?*

And Dan T., for sure you know more than you are telling me. Following the line of trees that Dan T. had taken, he could see the little man now dancing around a smoldering log. The ranger and Tilden could not see him from where they stood, below an outcropping of sandstone. Dan T. seemed to be weaving sign language in and out of the Wall of Smoke rising from the log. "*What a weird little devil you are,*" he thought.

The ranger and Tilden were now standing over the area in which the gun lay. *Maybe the guy tripped and shot himself with his own gun, weeks or months ago, while hunting, and nobody ever discovered it,* Miguel thought. *Unlikely, but possible. It is strange that no one so far is concerned with the remains of the dead cattle carcasses. There is no reason under the sun that they didn't run up the arroyo ahead of the fire. Well, yes, there is one. They were also dead like the man, if it is a man. I wonder which person killed the animals, the dead person or the person with the moccasins?* Too much for a man whose day began with a forest fire at 1 a.m.

Miguel began to doze off. His head jerked up as his chin touched the pointed corner of the federal report sticking out of the inside pocket of his uniform. Sitting there in the midst of nature's devastation and the cultural questions surrounding it, Miguel looked at the government report. Even before he read the first words, he saw a contrast between the crisp white paper and the charred background of a blackened hillside. He finished reading it and folded it back into his pocket. Jefferson had summarized the report correctly; murder and suicide. Tell that to the Navajo people back at the arroyo. He wouldn't even try.

"How long have you been standing there, you sneaky Indian?" Miguel turned around to see Dan T.

"Not long. You noticed the dead cattle? No? Maybe you asked why they did not run from the fire?" After years with Dan T., Miguel recognized that it was not really a question but a set up for Dan T. to expound. "I'll tell you the answer. See the overflow tank? It is poisoned with something. The birds, and now the rattlesnake, lie on top of the water dead, the snake fully extended. It escaped the fire but not its death, the same death as the cattle received from the water."

"Do you think that the poisoned water could explain the death of the person over there?"

The silence from Dan T. was more than the cultural extension of time. They looked at each other and he shook his head. "No. But I think that the dead one who lies over there is connected to the dead one who lies up there." Dan T pointed with the twisted motion of his lips and his bouncing head towards the mountaintop.

"What did you say? There is a dead man up there?" Miguel pulled his feet up under him. Looking across the arroyo at Tilden and the ranger, Dan T. slowly stiffened his hand and arm on Miguel's shoulder, keeping him seated on the log.

"Do not spread any alarm until you hear what I say. Yes, I find two men up above. Both sleeping; one the sleep of rest, the other the sleep of death. The one who will not awake is located at the site of an old Navajo sweat lodge. I know him as a firefighter. He is from Cuba. Both men, I am sure, stayed on the fire site to put out flare-ups. The dead one, I think, put out a flare-up that killed him. We don't want others into that site. I think that it still might kill."

Miguel remained quiet, trying to get a fix on what Dan T. was telling him. Dan T., trying to protect his words, turned away from the deputy and the ranger. "The water makes death. So, also, what was stored in the sweat lodge makes death when it burns. How do these two get to each other?"

Miguel knew the answer. Lodge Tom, according to the students, had emptied the contents of the aluminum case, probably in the holding tank, thinking that he was destroying some drugs that belonged to Cornell Sussman. "Dan T, I think I have the answer to the connecting question. The bigger questions, though, are what is the stuff and how did it get to Horse Mountain?" Yawning as though they were having a casual conversation, Miguel whispered, "You sit down, now, and wait for my signal."

Miguel took his time walking over to Tilden and the ranger, passing the charred remains. He decided to make them discover the dead firefighter. "Sam, don't you have some men working on the flare-ups? I'd like to ask a few questions about an explosion during the fire last night. Maybe they've seen something."

"Good idea. I know about where they are patrolling," Sam replied, eagerly taking the lead.

Miguel gave Dan T. the signal to join them. "I want Dan T. to compare any of your men's findings with the stories that he may have heard from his people last night." Dan T. realized immediately what Miguel was doing and began to wander in the direction of the dead firefighter. After fifteen minutes or so Dan T. came within sight of the dead man and startled everyone with his shouting. The sweat lodge was built near the ridge of a little rise. The firefighter lay across the burned logs of the small structure; face down in a pile of smoldering dust.

"Jesus, look it's Ted." Both Miguel and Dan T. grabbed the ranger as he moved toward the dead man. "Please wait, Mr. Perkins. Look closely. Something underneath, from below, killed him. See how he falls."

"Let go of me, you goddam Indian. How the hell do you know so much?" Miguel increased his grip on the ranger as Dan T. backed off.

Unaffected by the ranger's pushing him, Dan T. pointed to the dead man. "He was dead before hitting the ground. See, no shaking, no surprise, no tossing, and no disturbance in dust. I think that he breathed his death."

The tension in the ranger relaxed under Miguel's grip. "How the hell do I know but what you are saying could be true? OK. Let me get this information back to the station." He walked over to a clearing so that he could better see and describe to the station the scene in front of him.

"Miguel, what the fuck has hit us?" It wasn't a question but a conclusion that an immense tragedy was unfolding. Tilden turned to his radio to get the sheriff's office informed.

He looked at his watch and shook his head, realizing that the scheduled news conference was probably over by now.

Miguel and Dan T. left the scene to inform the Twin Rivers people.

CHAPTER 34

Saw Tooth
Late Thursday afternoon

By late Thursday afternoon, the US Forest Service, the Cuba County Sheriff's Department, and the Saw Tooth mayor had scheduled a joint news conference for 5:30 p.m. They would hold it on the top step of the terraced landscape surrounding the US Forest Service building. The organizers thought that in contrast to the subject of the conference, namely, fire and death, the peaceful atmosphere of pines and pinion might reduce some of the trauma everyone had experienced during the past few days.

Also, the natural stage would allow easy access to the many reporters and TV stations that the fire had brought to their small village. The mayor told the state police, who were keeping traffic moving on US Highway 50 amidst all of the vehicles going in and out of the fire scene, to be on the lookout for the two federal officers coming in from Twin Rivers. If possible, to let them know that they were wanted at the news conference. Jefferson and MacDonald got the message five times from five state police officers between Big Screw Canyon and the ranger's station.

By conference time, the size of the crowd necessitated a loudspeaker with its usual feedback and squeals. The number of presenters had grown as well, and now included a representative from the state police, a spokesperson from the Navajo Nation, Captain Tsosie and Cornell Sussman. The mayor, Roy Wilkins, set the tone for the conference with his opening statement. The long gangly Texan, who had moved to Saw Tooth after thirty-five years of police work in Amarillo, introduced himself and continued, "I want to congratulate the people of Saw Tooth for the manner in which they supported the large influx of people who worked on the fire out over there on the Twin River Reservation." Wilkins had his heart in the right place. He was still working on his geography.

For him, everything north of town belonged to the Indians. "Together, we saved that reservation. And I know how grateful those Navajos are. From what I can understand, they still got some mighty big problems up there. And that's why we got all of these people here on this stage. They are the ones who will get the job done for them. I am hoping that, by hearing from each of them, we can better learn what our part here in Saw Tooth will be for the future and we can give them our best cooperation. We just got to remember that those Indians are our neighbors.

"Now, there will be time for any questions after we have heard from everyone. The first person here is going to tell us about the fire on Horse Mountain. He needs no introduction, excepting those who don't know him. He is Bill Frost, district ranger for the US Forest Service, who comes from right here in the building behind us."

Weldon Prince surveyed the large gathering from the back of one of the pickup trucks that had been parked down in the ditch across the street from the ranger's station. Sitting in the bed of a truck was the standard bleacher for watching parades, baseball games, rodeos, and press conferences. Sussman, he thought, looked pretty good after last night's cocaine feast to celebrate a victory over the feds. Now, he wished that he had gone. Not far from Sussman was Rhonda.

Prince looked for a Twin Rivers Navajo in the crowd of people. Not one. To be honest, there was only one Navajo he was looking for...Dan T. The image of the pointed head and glassy eyes appearing over the tip of the hunting knife continued to haunt his every moment. A sleepless night did nothing for his self-control. In addition, all of the stories circulating in the town about the events surrounding the fire only complicated any possibilities for his immediate future.

Was there really a dead man found on the burned mountain? Was it Alquire's man or another Twin Rivers Navajo? Would he have a life without Alquire? Was the dead one the medicine man who had killed Lodge and Katy? Wait, wait. Listen, listen. He felt a strange compulsion, an anxious uncertainty, pumping into his veins with every pull of his diaphragm.

"The reason that the fire was controlled so quickly," the ranger was saying, "is that, between the Navajos on one side and the Saw Tooth people on the other, we kept it in the original fire line. Keeping the fire contained in that circle was just great work and not a little luck. Along with the mayor, I want to thank all of you for your selfless response. You just organized yourself in that first critical hour and got the job done. Now, that is the good news."

The ranger didn't want to approach the next subject. It was something that would certainly raise more questions than he had answers. "The bad news is that we found a body up there, badly burned. Identification is near impossible. That's how awful bad it is. I have a man on the scene and I know that the sheriff's deputy is also in there somewhere. The state's crime lab will be going back up into that area for the second time this week. Now, I know that you are all aware of the deaths of Lodge and Katy Tom, the two Indians from the reservation. The federal officers over there will update you on their investigation on the Twin Rivers. Also, I know that the sheriff will give you the latest word from Deputy Tilden about the burned body. While some are trying to connect the events on Horse Mountain with the Toms' deaths, I can assure you that there is no connection."

They are connected, you goddam fool. They are connected and unless you find the connection there will be more deaths, probably mine among them. Prince's mind was screaming every word. Fear of exposure about his involvement was restricting his breathing. Ever so slowly, it was becoming clear to him why the Indian policeman and Sussman were on the stage. Trying to look unconcerned, he climbed down from the pickup, and gradually moved across the street and toward the men on the top terrace.

The Ranger continued. "Now, the last thing, I know a lot of you, myself included, saw some moccasin tracks walking up the arroyo, away from the area of the windmill and into the Twin Rivers Reservation. How that someone could have walked away from the destruction of that fire, well, I must admit…it is…not a little strange…it is, in plain truth, eerie. It just spooked all of us for a while. I know that there is some logical and natural explanation."

The ranger backed away from the mike for a moment, nudged his hat with his forefinger and at the same time wet his thumb with his tongue. He then flipped several pages in his note book and after a moment continued.

"Also, there's the question of whether the cause of the fire connected to those moccasin feet. But right now, we are still looking for a connection. We have a lot of questions for the Twin Rivers People. Oh, one other thing…for the next couple of days, there will be several two-man teams making sure that no hot spots flare up again."

Prince blanched with anxiety at the image of the moccasin feet. *It was Alquire's Mexican Indian, you fucking buffoon! He is the one that killed the Toms. He is the one that got away, coming down the arroyo into the reservation to kill others.* Once again, resorting to pain for self-control, he leaned up against a tree and bit down on the bent knuckle of his forefinger until he could taste blood in his mouth. Unfortunately, the pain would not quell the flush of anger bursting in his head.

"Hey! Doc, sit down, will you? There is nobody sick up there." Everybody around Pat Wade's voice gave a little chuckle.

Prince ignored them and continued a more determined approach to the stage. *Little do they know.* Up closer now, Prince confirmed what he thought he'd seen from the pickup. *The goddam Indian up there is Dan T. It is not Captain Tsosie.* The cap could not cover the low hairline. Was he the only one who could see that pointed head and those glassy eyes? *The son of a bitch is going to tell everyone that I brought the bad medicine to Twin Rivers. And besides that, goddam Sussman is going to tell them that I fucked Katy.*

MacDonald was saying, "Willow Jr. and Woodson Pino have not been released. We still have some questions, in several areas. I want everyone to understand, however, that, even though our investigation is not complete, there is no suspect and that includes Willow and Woodson. They are not suspects. The killings could eventually be declared a murder and a suicide."

You should say no suspects yet. But if Dan T. gets to the microphone he will tell everyone. He will expose me as the suspect. The commotion around Prince was growing. He gave no attention to it. A few more feet and he could leap up and grab the cap off his head. *That will expose Dan T. as trying to impersonate Captain Tsosie. That will surely save me.*

MacDonald noticed the movement of the people off to his side but tried to continue, "What with the fire and the subsequent religious fervor of the Navajos caused by the moccasin feet, the logical thing for us to do is to put a little time between all these events and any further investigation. But I assure you, there is no wild killer on the loose. Lastly, I have sent another piece of potential evidence to the lab in Albuquerque. It is an aluminum suitcase. In this regard, we are hopeful that someone out there might give us a lead on that suitcase. Lodge Tom apparently found it on Horse Mountain last week. If you have any ideas about it, give your information to Deputy Tilden or the sheriff's department in Cuba."

As he was getting his final words out, "And don't forget, the Navajo Nation has a fine young police officer—" MacDonald saw the "stage" burst into action. Some people, including Sussman, were falling off the top of the terrace while others were scrambling to get up to that level. A state police officer was holding Weldon Prince's arm straight up in the air. Jefferson was prying open Prince's bloody fingers, one by one, trying to get a gun out of his hand. Prince had a knee on Captain Tsosie's neck.

The reference to a wild killer and the suitcase had brought Weldon Prince to the brink of his emotional stability. Jumping up the final two feet to the level of the speakers, Prince knocked the sheriff off his chair and grabbed his pistol from its holster. "That goddam Dan T. knows that the suitcase belongs to me," he shouted. In the commotion of bouncing bodies and chairs, the amplifier for the sound system went flying from the table next to the microphones.

With people pushing to get out of the way and others shouting to get to him, no one heard his cry, "You will tell no one, Dan T." He had the gun right on Captain Tsosie's temple and pulled the trigger, but it would not fire. Prince knew nothing about the gun's safety lock. In another instant, the state police officer had him hanging in the air while Jefferson held his wrist with the gun. Even in the pain of his twisted arm, Prince kept yelling at Captain Tsosie. "Dan T., they know all about you now. You can't get away acting like a cop. It is all on the camera for the nightly news." In that instant, on the terrace below them, the electrical system in the amplifier shorted out and sent up a wall of acrid smoke that engulfed Weldon Prince and his captors. Some Navajos later would say that it all coincided with Dan T.'s dance on Horse Mountain.

Prince's mad ravings continued until the Cuba sheriff left him handcuffed in the back seat of the van between two of his deputies. As the door slammed shut, Pat Wade thought he heard Prince yell, "Sussman, I lied! I did fuck her! It could have been my kid!"

The chaos ended the news conference. It would be another twenty-five minutes before news of Dan T.'s discovery of the dead firefighter would reach Saw Tooth.

CHAPTER 35

Robert's brush with death finally conquered him as he climbed, under the strength of Feather's lope, back up to the fence line, the boundary that he had crossed just two nights ago. Unable to keep his grip in the saddle, he slid out and fell to the ground, shivering and retching until he lost consciousness. As awareness returned, he realized that Feather stood over him. He grabbed the stirrup and pulled until he was able to reach the saddle horn. Opening the backpack that hung over the horn, he pulled out his canteen and drank it almost empty.

In frenzy, he tore the sweaty plastic shirt over his head. The fire on the mountain, directly in front of him, was beginning to register, but without any memory of his part in it. With shaking hands, he untied the elk skin from behind the saddle and threw it over his shoulders. He pulled himself close to Feather's neck for her warmth. She responded by stiffening under his weight.

After a moment, feeling returned to his feet and legs, and stability settled in. He looked up and over her hindquarters and finally became conscious of the enormous tongues of fire leaping from Horse Mountain into the night sky, losing themselves in clouds of billowing sparks and smoke. And now, for the first time, his mouth and throat tasted the death, the smoke, and the heat that he had so narrowly escaped.

His last awareness of the fire had been during his run in the arroyo, to outdistance the grass fire, and then, finally, his jump up on the sloping ground to skirt around the fire to the west. After that, he fell into a trot all the way to Donkey Springs, aware of the fire only as a growing glare on the other side of the bluffs between Horse Mountain and himself. He had found Feather without any trouble, untied the rope, and led her to the tree that held the saddle and the elk skin. Needing no urging from him, Feather had galloped away from the smoke and fire for a mile or better and only stopped as her rider's weight began to leave the saddle.

Now, with his strength returning he walked with Feather along the fence line, grateful that he was going away from the death and destruction lying behind him. His mind returned to the Hogan and the instruction to build a fire on Horse Mountain; a fire to burn the evil one. He thought, *whatever it meant to Grandfather, the fire was my only chance for survival.* Below and to the east, he could see the line of lights leaving various side roads and congesting the main road up to Horse Mountain. Some of them then eventually turned off onto the dirt roads between the fire and the reservation.

When he reached the mesa overlooking North Chapel, he again got up into the saddle. Instead of giving Feather her head and going down the mesa, Robert pulled her left, up the mesa and into the direction of the Continental Mountains. He let Feather walk freely until the dawn appeared at his back. At that point, he stepped from the saddle and decided that he would stay where he was until nightfall. Loosening the saddle and tying Feather to a bush, he dropped to the ground from total exhaustion. He crawled to the nearest pinion and slept in the comfort of the elk skin.

It was a dream that returned him to the hunt. He was tracking Lodge and Katy straight up the side of a mountain, getting closer and closer, until he could hear Katy's screams. When he finally had them in his bow sight, an old man came out of the bushes and told him that he had won the game. As a good child, he should give the bow to Lodge this time and let him be the hunter.

When Robert refused to give up the bow, the old man put him in the Hogan and nailed the door shut. Jaime broke through the roof to free him, but the old man caught them and, as punishment, he set the Hogan on fire. The smoke from the Hogan's fire had a dead man floating in it. After Robert awoke, for a very long moment he stayed in the fire, only because he could actually see smoke angling overhead and tailing off to the north. The dead man, however, had disappeared in the daylight, but not from his thoughts.

Shaking his sleepiness, Robert was now reliving those moments near the pond before leaping into the tank. How many times could he have hit a moving target at that distance? *Hardly ever. If it had not had that wolf's head,* Robert thought, *I could never have released the arrow.* In that flash of instinct, the wolf's appearance and the Wall of Smoke had clouded out the fact that there almost certainly was a man beneath it. But the question would not leave him. *Was it his will to kill the animal with the deadly arrow, or was it his self-defense reaction against a man who had taken five shots at him?* There was another possibility: that the skin walker was an evil spirit and had somehow been both man and beast. In Grandfather's words, "Let the spirit of your father guide you to the evil one...kill it...burn it." Had the spirit of John Sedillo dominated the moment?

Looking back to Horse Mountain, he no longer saw the billowing clouds, but rather wispy streaks of smoke rising into the sky. His heart filled with gratitude that the destruction had stopped. It would be a good three-hour ride to get down off the mesa. If he left as darkness fell, he should be at the Hogan well before midnight. He had never experienced such hunger and thirst as he did now.

CHAPTER 36

North Chapel
Thursday night

When Tanya brought the old man his food during the day, Grandfather would not allow her to stay or speak of any news. He followed the progress of the fire only when he had to go out and relieve himself. Otherwise, he kept his vigil before the Wall of Smoke.

Milton arrived before dusk each evening, bringing more wood. They would not speak, communicating only, for an hour or two, by their presence. Tonight, however, Milton stayed. They prayed that the light from Horse Mountain had cleansed their land of the bad blood.

As was the case with all the women on the reservation, Tanya kept her vigil for the menfolk when they were out at night. She sat in her chair before the open doorway watching, waiting, thinking. The man/child dangled his legs through the planks of the wooden fence. Looking forward to Feather's return, he had water and grain sitting at the edge of the pickup's tailgate and a bale of hay in the corral. Both had kept the same vigil last night for the Hunter's return.

Lost in her deep concerns about Robert's connection with the stories of the remains found on Horse Mountain and with the moccasin feet running from the fire through the reservation arroyo, Tanya was startled from her reverie when Miguel's van entered the yard and Dan T. got out.

Neither of them has any right being here, she thought. *Ignorance might excuse Miguel, but Dan T. knows what is happening. I even told him as much, and surely he sees Milton's truck parked back by the ceremonial Hogan.*

"Dan T., what are you doing—" Tanya's anger stopped as Dan T. put up a bloody palm, extended it to within inches of her face. "Much more of our people's blood may be shed." The words came through sobs and tears. "Tell Grandfather that Miguel and I must join his council."

"Dan T, you know that the white man is forbidden—"

Dan T., shaking as though in a convulsion, placed the tip of the bloody knife across his palm and again drew blood; this time, a lot of blood. Then, in a whispered voice of desperation said, "Tell him how I come, in blood and tears."

Tanya, reeling from the strangeness in Dan T.'s actions, went to the Hogan, and returned with Milton. Miguel, after telling the boy/man something, joined Tanya and waited as Dan T. and Milton spoke in whispers. As Dan T. knelt down and brought his hands from the earth to his head, Miguel knew he was describing the death that comes from below. Dan T. rose, keeping his mud-clotted hand away from his pants, looked at Miguel, and all four proceeded to the Hogan.

"Together, Grandfather," Dan T. began, "Miguel and I bring you our stories." Dan T. now spoke with the authority of the medicine man that he never became. "The stories shall start before Lodge and Katy's death and end with our presence here. Some of our story is what we do not know. We trust that you can tell us these parts." The elders assumed their position behind the Wall of Smoke; Tanya, Dan T, and Miguel on the opposite side. The content of their stories was to be placed in the context of the ancient ones; all would hear and judge.

"Grandfather," Miguel began at Dan T.'s nod, "I am honored to be in your council, but I am deeply saddened at the words that I must bring you. First, what Lodge does. In the week preceding the deaths of Lodge and Katy, it appears that Lodge discovered one or more aluminum suitcases on or near Horse Mountain. He believed that the suitcase and its contents belonged to Cornell Sussman. It also appears that he believed the contents to be illegal drugs. He destroyed the contents by dumping and dissolving them in the watering trough just below the windmill on Horse Mountain. The federal officer and I found the suitcase in Lodge's office. Mr. Wade's students told us about Lodge's thoughts. We have seen proof of Lodge's actions."

Miguel's audience remained motionless. After shifting his weight to his other knee, he continues. "Then Lodge and Katy's bodies are found. As you know, Woodson discovered them early Monday. Our investigation has continued for four days. What I have now to tell you, I know that you will not believe. Tanya has told us so. But, based upon the evidence at the crime scene and the stories of the witnesses we have interviewed, it appears that Lodge shot Katy and then shot himself."

Miguel would have felt better if grandfather and Tanya jumped at him. Their stoicism made him feel creepy and wonder if he should go on. He quickly finished. "Now, it does also appear that someone else was in the house and moved the bodies after their deaths. It could be Woodson. However, his clothing did not indicate that he did it. Also, his physical condition makes it highly unlikely. We have no suspects."

Sitting back on his haunches, Miguel looked at Dan T. Grandfather, sensing that Dan T. was about to tell his story, reached for another limb to place on the fire.

Choosing to kneel, Dan T. began. "I, too, will start with the suitcase. Grandfather, I know that the suitcase comes to the reservation in the hands of the white doctor. He would take them to the house of my uncle, Fred Abeyta, and there, the Mexican would take them and, it seems, hide them in Horse Mountain. Many times, my uncle told me about the doctor, Weldon Prince.

"Recently, I saw the fear of death in the white doctor's eyes. During the meeting of the white men, I put the suitcase in his hands and he screamed for his life. Grandfather, Lodge Tom was wrong about the suitcases. They did not contain drugs for white men. Rather, the suitcases hold a terrible and quick death. A death that is delivered in water. A death that is delivered in the air when it burns. Many cattle, the bird, and the snake die when they drink the poisoned water from the drinking tank at the windmill.

Dan T. edged closer to fire and looked at it as though what he was saying was actually pictured in the smoke. "And now, I bring more bad news. A firefighter on Horse Mountain dies when he breathes the smoke of the same poison. Miguel and I were on Horse Mountain to see it. We see the water, we see the dead firefighter, we see the burned remains of the one I believe to be the Mexican from my uncle's place. This we learned only an hour ago. We come directly to you. Our stories are true."

After adding another limb to the fire, the old man spoke. "We will say nothing more until the Hunter returns and speaks. Tanya, you return to your vigil. We must wait and—" It never once occurred to Grandfather that Robert could be the dead man whose ashes are on Horse Mountain.

∽

Shortly after leaving the Hogan , the click of stone upon stone jolted Tanya, pushing her, once again, from her vigil at the door to the stove where she had kept warm for these many hours, making the fried bread, the chili stew, and the coffee. Francis John II was waiting for her outside the door with a pail of water, and together, their hands full of what they felt would be required for the return of the Hunter and his horse, they walked to the ceremonial Hogan.

Eventually, the sound of the horse on the rocky trail turned into the silhouetted images of the horse and its rider, shadowed in the wrap of an elk skin. Finally, the images turned into the reality of a haggard Hunter and a beaten horse whose head now hung in Francis John II's arms, drinking deeply from the cool water.

The Hunter dismounted very slowly and deliberately entered the Hogan and walked through the Wall of Smoke to his former position. The robe fell from his shoulders and lay across his legs. He raised his head and immediately felt that all of his efforts were in vain when he saw those who now sat around the fire. Grandfather Tom, Milton, and Tanya near him. On the other side of the Wall of Smoke were Dan T. and Miguel.

Grandfather Tom began. "I am sorry, Robert, that you cannot take your rest at this moment. There are many evil things still unfolding upon the people this night. That is why Miguel and Dan T. are here. Do not be afraid. Now, tell us the story of Horse Mountain."

Robert detailed every step in his hunt, from the moment that he left the Hogan until his return. He emphasized that he started the fire to save his life from someone who had shot to kill him. He took them back to the flames and the Wall of Smoke on the side of Horse Mountain where the skin walker burst through the scourging façade of searing heat. In that instant of recognition, he had put an arrow in flight that had pierced the burning skin walker. The continued screeches of pain emanating from the tumbling figure signaled that the arrow had not found a vital organ and that death had delivered all of its agonies in the form of heat, smoke, burning flesh, and loss of blood from severed internal arteries. Even with his head underwater in order to escape the flames, the sounds of dying were still audible as if the very earth transmitted them.

"As you said, Grandfather, I then found Katy's blanket in the water and threw it on the fence when I ran from the fire, down the arroyo on my way to Donkey Springs and Feather. I rested this day on the mesa."

Everyone spoke at once. Grandfather stood. Silence returned. His shadow, cast from the fire onto the wall, loomed over the small band of reservation leaders. He spoke with finality and certainty, "Robert, You have killed the Bad Blood murderer of Lodge and Katy." Uncertain of his next move, Miguel remained silent.

Just then, the unlatched door of the Hogan suddenly banged against the log wall as the boy/man burst into the room, shouting, "Miguel, the box speaks; Miguel, the box speaks." Miguel calmed everyone by telling them that he told Francis John II to listen for messages on the van's radio. Miguel and Tanya left the Hogan.

When Miguel reached the sheriff's office in Saw Tooth on the radio, he was completely unprepared for the voice that answered. "Miguel, this is Jefferson. Listen very carefully. The governor of New Mexico has ordered the National Guard to surround the Twin Rivers Reservation. No one can go in or out. Also, the Guard has been authorized by the president to enter the reservation and to seal off Horse Mountain. The jurisdiction of the Tribal Police has been suspended. The material that killed the firefighter is a deadly chemical, as yet unidentified. Several animal deaths northeast of the fire are believed to be associated with the fire.

"I repeat, the Reservation's Wall of Smoke has carried something with it. Neither the county's emergency response teams nor any of the personnel at the university's firefighting and borderland security programs are equipped to extract the material from the site. Within an hour, I will be leaving to set up a command and control center at the Chapter House. Be there. Out."

Miguel frantically responded, "Jefferson, wait. The watering tank near the Windmill. I think that it also has been contaminated by the same chemicals." The connection had gone dead. He was uncertain if Jefferson heard him.

For a moment Miguel stood by the Suburban's door. Slowly, he walked over and sat with Tanya on the porch steps. In the silence, he tried to collect his thoughts. He pondered just how he would bring this latest news to the elders of Twin Rivers Reservation. The moonlight shadowed the slumping figure. Tanya began yet another vigil.

Made in the USA
Charleston, SC
01 November 2012